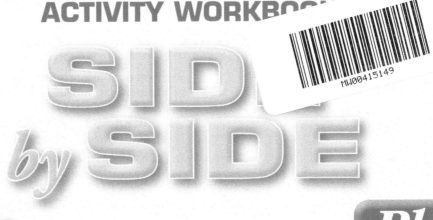

ACTIVITY WORKBOOK
SIDE by SIDE
Plus

Steven J. Molinsky • Bill Bliss

with

Carolyn Graham • Peter S. Bliss

Contributing Authors

Dorothy Lynde • Elizabeth Handley

Illustrated by

Richard E. Hill

TO THE TEACHER

Side by Side Plus Activity Workbook 1 provides supplemental activities to accompany *Side by Side Plus Student Book 1*. The all-skills activities include listening comprehension practice, GrammarRaps, and GrammarSongs featured on the included Digital Audio CDs. New material in this edition includes activities to support the Student Book Gazette lessons and a new workbook section offering focused practice with lifeskill competencies and employment topics. An integrated numeracy curriculum provides practice with numbers, basic math, and word problems. A complete Answer Key enables students to use the Workbook independently for self-study.

(*Side by Side Plus Test Prep Workbook 1*, available separately, offers test preparation practice through achievement tests for all units of the program. The tests are also available as reproducibles included with *Side by Side Plus Teacher's Guide 1*.)

Side by Side Plus Activity Workbook 1

Copyright © 2016 by Pearson Education, Inc.
All rights reserved.
No part of this publication may be reproduced, stored in a retrieval system, or transmitted in any form or by any means, electronic, mechanical, photocopying, recording, or otherwise, without the prior permission of the publisher.

Pearson Education, 10 Bank Street, White Plains, NY 10606

Staff credits: The people who make up the *Side by Side Plus* team, representing content creation, design, manufacturing, marketing, multimedia, project management, publishing, rights management, and testing are Pietro Alongi, Allen Ascher, Rhea Banker, Elizabeth Barker, Lisa Bayrasli, Elizabeth Carlson, Jennifer Castro, Tracey Munz Cataldo, Diane Cipollone, Aerin Csigay, Victoria Denkus, Dave Dickey, Daniel Dwyer, Wanda España, Oliva Fernandez, Warren Fischbach, Pam Fishman, Nancy Flaggman, Patrice Fraccio, Irene Frankel, Aliza Greenblatt, Lester Holmes, Janet Johnston, Caroline Kasterine, Barry Katzen, Ray Keating, Renee Langan, Jaime Lieber, José Antonio Méndez, Julie Molnar, Pamela Pia, Stuart Radcliffe, Jennifer Raspiller, Kriston Reinmuth, Mary Perrotta Rich, Tania Saiz-Sousa, Katherine Sullivan, Paula Van Ells, Kenneth Volcjak, Paula Williams, and Wendy Wolf.

Text composition: TSI Graphics, Inc.

Illustrations: Richard E. Hill

The authors gratefully acknowledge the contribution of Tina Carver in the development of the original *Side by Side* program.

ISBN-10: 0-13-418681-8
ISBN-13: 978-0-13-418681-8

Printed in the United States of America

Contents

A WHAT ARE THEY SAYING?

what's	is	my	from	name	phone number
where	are	your	I'm	address	

1. ___What's___ your name?

My __name__ is Janet Miller.

2. What's your __address__?

__My__ address __is__ 456 Main Street.

3. What's __your__ phone number?

My __phone number__ is 654-3960.

4. What's __your__ name?

My __name__ is Ken Green.

5. __what's__ your address?

My __address__ is 15 Park Street.

6. What's your __phone__ number?

__My__ phone __number__ is 379-1029.

7. __where__ __are__ you from?

__I'm__ __from__ Detroit.

B NAME/ADDRESS/PHONE NUMBER

STUDENT IDENTIFICATION CARD

Name: _Maria_ _Gonzalez_
             First Name   Last Name

Address: _235 Main Street_

           Bronx, New York

Phone
Number: _741-8906_

My name is Maria Gonzalez.
My address is 235 Main Street.
My phone number is 741-8906.

How about you? What's YOUR name, address, and phone number?

STUDENT IDENTIFICATION CARD

Name: _____
       First Name   Last Name

Address: _____

          _____

Phone
Number: _____

My name _____ ....

....

My _____ _____ ....

....

My _____ _____ _____

....

C LISTENING

Listen and circle the number you hear.

1. (5) / 9

2. 3 / 7

3. 1 / 2

4. 6 / 3

5. 4 / 1

6. 3 / 6

7. 5 / 4

8. 8 / 2

9. 10 / 0

10. 5 / 9

D NUMBERS

zero	0
one	1
two	2
three	3
four	4
five	5
six	6
seven	7
eight	8
nine	9
ten	10

Write the number.

four	4
seven	7
one	1
eight	8
ten	10
two	2
nine	9
six	6
five	5
three	3

Write the word.

6	six
2	two
7	seven
3	three
1	one
8	eight
10	ten
4	four
9	nine
5	five

E LISTENING 🔊

Listen and write the missing numbers.

1.
What's your phone number?
My phone number is 389-793 _2_ .

2. What's your telephone number?
My telephone number is 837-29___3.

3. What's your apartment number?
My apartment number is ___-B.

4. What's your address?
My address is ___ Main Street.

5. What's your fax number?
My fax number is 654-___ ___15.

6. What's your license number?
My license number is 26___3___9___ .

Listen and write the missing letters.

1. C-A-_R_-T-___-R

2. J-O-___-N-___-O-___

3. ___-E-R-___-L-___

4. A-N-D-E-___-S-___-N

5. ___-H-I-L-___-I-P

6. ___-A-R-___-I-N-E-___

G WHAT ARE THEY SAYING?

name	meet	you	Hi	Nice

A. Hello. My ____name____ ¹ is Dan Harris.

B. ___Hi___ ². I'm Susan Wilson.

Nice to ___meet___ ³ you.

A. ___Nice___ ⁴ to meet ___you___ ⁵, too.

is	you	Hello	I'm	My	to

A. Hi. ___My___ ⁶ name ___is___ ⁷ Alice Lane.

B. ___Hello___ ⁸. ___I'm___ ⁹ Bob Chang.

A. Nice ___to___ ¹⁰ meet you.

B. Nice to meet ___you___ ¹¹, too.

H GRAMMARRAP: *Hi! Hello!*

Listen. Then clap and practice.

A.   Hi.   I'm Jack.

B. Hello.   I'm Jill.

C.   Hi.   I'm Mary.

D. Hello.   I'm Bill.

All.   Nice to meet you.

    Nice to   meet you, too.

A.   Hi.   I'm Bob.

B. Hello.   I'm Tim.

C.   Hi.   I'm Susie.

D. Hello.   I'm Jim.

All.   Nice to   meet you.

    Nice to   meet you, too.

A PUZZLE

Across

1.
5.
6.
8.
10.
12.

Down

1.
2.
3.
4.
7.
8.
9.
11.

(crossword grid)

Across/Down answers shown in grid:
1 DICTIONARY
2 RULER
3 WALL
4 TABLE
5 CHAIR
6 BOOKSHELF
7 CLOCK
8 PENCIL
9 NOTEBOOK
10 GLOBE
11 MAP
12 BOARD

Cock Clock

B LISTENING

Listen and put a check (✓) under the correct picture.

1. ✔ ___   2. ___ ___   3. ___ ___

4. ___ ___   5. ___ ___   6. ___ ___

WHAT ARE THEY SAYING?

I'm	are	basement	attic	living room
we're	where	dining room	yard	~~bedroom~~
they're	you	kitchen	bathroom	

1. _Where_ are you?

   _I'm_ in the _bedroom_.

2. Where ___is___ Susan and Joe?

   _____ in the _____.

3. Where _____ you and Julie?

   _____ in the _____.

4. _Where_ are you?

   _I'm_ in the _____.

5. _____ _____ Ben and Maria?

   _____ in the _____.

6. Where _____ you and Betty?

   _____ in the _attic_.

7. _____ _____ Pam and Peter?

   _____ in the _____.

8. _____ _____ you?

   _____ in the _____.

D WHAT ARE THEY SAYING?

where's	she's	classroom	garage	he's	living room	it's

1. _____Where's_____ David?

___He's___ in the __garage__ .

2. __Where's__ Millie?

__She's__ in the __living room__ .

3. __Where's__ the computer?

__It's__ in the __classroom__ .

E WHERE ARE THEY?

we	he	they
	she	
	it	

(Mr. and Mrs. Chen) 1. _____They_____ are in the kitchen.

(Ms. Carter) 2. _____She_____ is in the dining room.

(Mr. Grant) 3. _____He_____ is in the bathroom.

(Harry and Mary) 4. _____They_____ are in the basement.

(Ellen and I) 5. _____We_____ are in the attic.

(The bookshelf) 6. _____It_____ is in the living room.

(Mr. White) 7. _____He_____ is in the garage.

(Mrs. Miller) 8. _____She_____ is in the classroom.

(The telephone book) 9. _____It_____ is in the bedroom.

F WHERE ARE THEY?

I'm	we're	he's	where's
	you're	she's	
	they're	it's	

(He is) 1. _____He's_____ in the bedroom.

(They are) 2. _____They're_____ in the basement.

(We are) 3. _____We're_____ in the attic.

(I am) 4. _____I'm_____ in the bathroom.

(It is) 5. _____It's_____ in the dining room.

(She is) 6. _____She's_____ in the living room.

(You are) 7. _____You're_____ in the garage.

(Where is) 8. _____Where's_____ the cell phone?

G THE BAKER FAMILY

The Baker family is at home today. **(1)** Mrs. Baker is ___in___ ___the___ ___living___ ___room___. **(2)** Mr. Baker is _____ _____ _____. **(3)** Peggy and Jim are _____ _____ _____. **(4)** Kevin is _____ _____ _____. **(5)** Susie is _____ _____ _____. **(6)** And the car is _____ _____ _____.

H WHERE ARE THEY?

he's	they're
she's	
it's	

1. Where's Mrs. Baker?   _She's in the living room._

2. Where's Mr. Baker?   _____

3. Where are Peggy and Jim?   _____

4. Where's Kevin?   _____

5. Where's Susie?   _____

6. Where's the car?   _____

❶ WHAT'S THE SIGN?

Fill in the signs. Then complete the sentences.

1. Helen is _____ in the park _____ .

2. Mr. and Mrs. Grant are _____ _____ .

3. Edward is _____ .

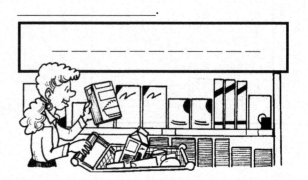

4. Maria is _____ .

5. Jim and Sarah are _____ _____ .

6. Billy is _____ .

7. The monkey is _____ .

8. Ms. Johnson is _____ .

10   Activity Workbook

J LISTENING

Listen and write the number under the correct picture.

_____

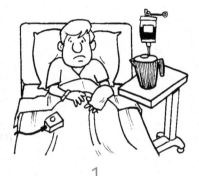

_1_

_____

_____

_____

_____

K LISTENING

Listen and circle the word you hear.

1. zoo （you）
2. Ms. Mr.
3. We're They're
4. Where How
5. Where Where's
6. She's He's
7. on in
8. Is It's

L MATCHING

Match the nationality and the city.

_c_ 1. We're Mexican. We're from _____.

____ 2. She's Greek. She's from _____.

____ 3. He's Chinese. He's from _____.

____ 4. I'm Italian. I'm from _____.

____ 5. They're Puerto Rican. They're from _____.

____ 6. We're Korean. We're from _____.

____ 7. She's Japanese. She's from _____.

a. Shanghai

b. San Juan

c. Mexico City

d. Seoul

e. Athens

f. Tokyo

g. Rome

Activity Workbook **11**

M GrammarRap: *Where's Jack?*

Listen. Then clap and practice.

A. Where's   Jack?

B.   He's in the   kitchen.

A. Where's   Jill?

B.   She's in the   dining room.

A. Where's   Mom?

B.   She's in the   living room.

A. Where's   Fred?   Fred's in   bed.

All.   Fred's in   bed.

       Fred's in   bed.

A.   Jack's in the   kitchen.

All.   Fred's in   bed.

A.   Jack's in the   kitchen.

B.   Jill's in the   dining room.

A.   Mom's in the   living room.

All.   Fred's in   bed.

N GrammarRap: *Where Are Fred and Mary?*

Listen. Then clap and practice.

Where are	Fred and Mary

A.	Where's	Jack?	A.	Jack and	Jill.
B.	Where's	Jill?	B.	Betty and	Bill.
C.	Where are Fred and Mary?		C.	Bob and	Lou.
D.	Where's	Bill?	D.	Mary and	Sue.
A.	Where's	Ed?	A.	Jack and	Jill.
B.	Where's	Sue?	B.	Betty and	Bill.
C.	Where are Bob and	Betty?	C.	Bob and	Lou.
D.	Where are Tom and Lou?		D.	Mary and	Sue.

doing	watching	I'm	we're	you
reading	sleeping	he's	they're	what
playing	eating	she's	are	what's
studying	cooking			

STUDENT BOOK
PAGES **17–24**

1. _____What_____ are you doing?

I'm _____studying_____ English.

2. What's Carla _____doing_____?

_____She's_____ _____eating_____.

3. _____What's_____ Walter doing?

He's _____sleeping_____.

4. _____What_____ _____are_____ Julie and David doing?

_____They're_____ _____reading_____ the newspaper.

5. _____What_____ _____are_____ you and George doing?

_____We're_____ _____watching_____ TV.

6. _____What_____ _____are_____ you _____doing_____?

_____I'm_____ _____playing_____ the piano.

7. _____What's_____ William doing?

_____He's_____ _____cooking_____ dinner.

H. MN

B WHAT ARE THEY DOING?

cooking	eating	playing	singing	studying	watching
drinking	listening	reading	sleeping	teaching	

1. He's _____eating_____ breakfast.

2. She's _____ milk.

3. They're _____ mathematics.

4. He's _____ the newspaper.

5. They're _____.

6. She's _____.

7. He's _____ to music.

8. They're _____ TV.

9. She's _____ dinner.

10. He's _____.

11. They're _____ baseball.

B **14** Activity Workbook

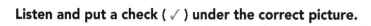

C LISTENING

Listen and put a check (✓) under the correct picture.

1. ✔ _____   2. _____ _____

3. _____ _____   4. _____ _____

5. _____ _____   6. _____ _____

7. _____ _____   8. _____ _____

9. _____ _____   10. _____ _____

D GRAMMARRAP: *Frank?! At the Bank?!*

Listen. Then clap and practice.

A. Where's   Frank?

B. He's working at the   bank.

A.   Frank?!   At the bank?!

B.   Yes, that's   right.

He's working at the   bank.

All.   Frank?!   At the bank?!   Oh,   no!

A. Where's   Sue?

B. She's working at the   zoo.

A.   Sue?!   At the zoo?!

B.   Yes, that's   right.

She's working at the   zoo.

All.   Sue?!   At the zoo?!   Oh,   no!

A. Where's   Paul?

B. He's working at the   mall.

A.   Paul?!   At the mall?!

B.   Yes, that's   right.

He's working at the   mall.

All.   Paul?!   At the mall?!   Oh,   no!

E WHAT'S THE QUESTION?

Where is	{ he / she / it } ?		What's	{ he / she / it } doing?
Where are	{ you / they } ?		What are	{ you / they } doing?

1. Where are you ? — I'm in the garage.

2. What's he doing ? — He's cooking dinner.

3. _____ ? — They're in the park.

4. _____ ? — We're playing with the dog.

5. _____ ? — He's in the attic.

6. _____ ? — She's listening to the radio.

7. _____ ? — She's in the yard.

8. _____ ? — We're at the beach.

9. _____ ? — He's sleeping.

10. _____ ? — It's in the classroom.

11. _____ ? — They're eating lunch.

12. _____ ? — I'm in the hospital.

F GRAMMARRAP: *Eating Lunch*

Listen. Then clap and practice.

What's he	Where are	What are

A. Where's Charlie?

B. He's in the kitchen.

A. What's he doing?

B. Eating lunch.

All. Charlie's in the kitchen eating lunch.

Charlie's in the kitchen eating lunch.

A. Who's in the kitchen?

B. Charlie's in the kitchen.

A. What's he doing?

B. Eating lunch.

A. Where's Betty?

B. She's in the bedroom.

A. What's she doing?

B. Reading a book.

All.   Betty's in the   bedroom   reading a   book.

Betty's in the   bedroom   reading a   book.

A.   Who's in the   bedroom?

B.   Betty's in the   bedroom.

A.   What's she   doing?

B.   Reading a   book.

A.   Where are Mom and   Dad?

B.   They're in the   living room.

A.   What are they   doing?

B.   Watching Channel   Seven.

All.   Betty's in the   bedroom.

Mom's in the   living room.

Dad's in the   living room.

Charlie's in the   kitchen.

A.   Where's   Charlie?

All.   He's in the   kitchen.

A.   What's he   doing?

All.   Eating   lunch.

✓ CHECK-UP TEST: Chapters 1–3

A. Answer the questions.

Ex. What's your telephone number?

My ....telephone number is 567-1032...

1. What's your name?

    ....

2. What's your address?

    ....

3. Where are you from?

    ....

B. Circle the correct answer.

Ex. The map is on the
yard
(wall) .
park

1. We're eating
milk
cards .
lunch

2. What
Where's Ben doing?
What's

3. Max is
planting flowers
swimming in
singing

the bathroom.

4. Ms. Park is teaching
dinner
mathematics .
the radio.

5. Nice to
hello
hi you.
meet

6. The
pencil
attic is in the classroom.
shower

C. Fill in the blanks.

Ex. ___What's___ Bill doing?

1. Maria is _____ the hospital.

2. I'm _____ the newspaper.

3. Where's Joe? _____ in the cafeteria.

4. They're _____ TV.

5. What are you and Peter doing? _____ reading.

6. _____ the car? It's in the garage.

7. What are you _____? I'm studying.

8. Where's the cell phone? _____ in the basement.

9. _____ are Mr. and Mrs. Chen doing?

10. Carol _____ Bob are eating breakfast.

D. Listen and write the letter or number you hear.

Ex. M-A-R-_K_

1. C-A-R-___-E-R

2. 354-9___12

3. 890-74___2

4. ___-U-L-I-E

5. 6___2-3059

6. 517-___349

A FACT FILE: Titles

Choose the correct words.

1. He's our English teacher. His name is (Mr.) / Ms. Parker.

2. Mrs. / Mr. Harper is in the yard. She's planting flowers.

5. She's our mathematics teacher. Her name is Ms. / Mr. Wu.

4. What's Mr. / Miss Grant doing? She's eating dinner.

5. His name is Mr. / Ms. David Cutler.

B FACT FILE: What's the Nickname?

Match the names and the nicknames.

_e_	1. Peter	a.	Sue	___	6. James	f.	Bob
___	2. Judith	b.	Tom	___	7. Patricia	g.	Jim
___	3. Thomas	c.	Kate	___	8. Robert	h.	Betty
___	4. Katherine	d.	Judy	___	9. William	i.	Patty
___	5. Susan	e.	Pete	___	10. Elizabeth	j.	Bill

C BUILD YOUR VOCABULARY! Categories

Write these words in the correct categories.

basketball	clarinet	tic tac toe
checkers	soccer	trumpet
chess	tennis	violin

Sports	Instruments	Games
basketball	_____	_____
_____	_____	_____
_____	_____	_____

D BUILD YOUR VOCABULARY! Crossword

Across

4.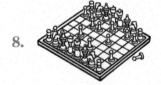

⁴C L A R I N E T

6.

7.

8.

Down

1.

2.

3.

5.

E "CAN-DO" REVIEW

Match the "can do" statement and the correct sentence.

_j_	1. I can say my name.	a. 1430 Central Avenue.
____	2. I can greet people.	b. I'm Japanese.
____	3. I can give my address.	c. Where's the ruler?
____	4. I can give my telephone number.	d. I'm studying.
____	5. I can ask the location of objects.	e. Nice to meet you.
____	6. I can give my location.	f. I'm from Beirut.
____	7. I can give my nationality.	g. I'm in the living room.
____	8. I can tell where I'm from.	h. (415) 628–1539.
____	9. I can tell about my current activities.	i. It's a beautiful day!
____	10. I can describe the weather.	j. My name is Emerita.

what	my	our	cleaning	apartment
what's	his	their	doing	children
are	her		fixing	homework
				sink

1. Hi! _____What's_____ Jason doing?

He's _____

_____ room.

2. What's Peggy _____?

She's _____

_____ car.

3. _____ are you doing?

I'm cleaning _____

_____.

4. What are your _____ doing?

They're doing _____

_____.

5. What _____ you doing?

We're fixing _____ _____.

Activity Workbook   **21**

B WHAT'S THE WORD?

my	his	her	its	our	your	their

1. I'm feeding ____my____ cat.

2. We're washing _____ clothes.

3. They're painting _____ bedroom.

4. She's fixing _____ sink.

5. It's eating _____ dinner.

6. You're cleaning _____ yard.

7. He's reading _____ e-mail.

C LISTENING

Listen and circle the word you hear.

1. your   (our)   3. her   his   5. your   our

2. his   her   4. our   their   6. my   its

D PUZZLE

Across

1. I'm painting _____ apartment.

3. We're fixing _____ TV.

6. Bobby and Tim are cleaning _____ room.

7. Bill is doing _____ homework.

Down

2. You're doing _____ exercises.

4. The dog is eating _____ dinner.

5. Ruth is brushing _____ teeth.

$$\text{Yes, I am.} \quad \text{Yes,} \left\{ \begin{array}{c} \text{he} \\ \text{she} \\ \text{it} \end{array} \right\} \text{is.} \quad \text{Yes,} \left\{ \begin{array}{c} \text{we} \\ \text{you} \\ \text{they} \end{array} \right\} \text{are.}$$

1. A. Is Harry feeding his cat?

   B. _Yes,_ _he_ _is._

2. A. Are you and Tom cleaning your yard?

   B. _____ _____ _____

3. A. Is Mrs. Chen doing her exercises?

   B. _____ _____ _____

4. A. Are your children brushing their teeth?

   B. _____ _____ _____

5. A. Is George sleeping?

   B. _____ _____ _____

6. A. Is Irene planting flowers?

   B. _____ _____ _____

7. A. Are you washing your windows?

   B. _____ _____ _____

8. A. Am I in the hospital?

   B. _____ _____ _____

F GRAMMARRAP: *Busy! Busy! Busy!*

Listen. Then clap and practice.

What are	Is he	Yes, he	What's he

A. Are you busy?

B. Yes, I am.

A. What are you doing?

B. I'm talking to Sam.

A. Is he busy?

B. Yes, he is.

A. What's he doing?

B. He's talking to Liz.

A. Are they busy?

B. Yes, they are.

A. What are they doing?

B. They're washing their car.

All. I'm talking to Sam.

He's talking to Liz.

They're washing their car.

They're busy!

G LISTENING

Listen and circle the word you hear.

1. (he's)   she's   3. feeding   eating   5. our   their

2. his   her   4. apartment   yard   6. washing   watching

 24   Activity Workbook

H WHAT ARE THEY DOING?

1. He's _____washing_____ his hair.

2. They're _____ their yard.

3. We're _____ our exercises.

4. I'm _____ my e-mail.

5. She's _____ her living room.

6. You're _____ your cat.

I WHAT'S THE WORD?

Circle the correct words.

1. (They're) / Their washing they're / their windows.

2. Where / We're are Mr. and Mrs. Tanaka?

3. He's / His doing he's / his exercises.

4. Where are / Where's the cell phone?

5. We're brushing are / our teeth.

6. His / Is Richard busy?

7. What are / our you doing?

8. The cat is eating it's / its dinner.

laundromat	doing	playing	they're	what's	her	are
library	eating	reading	he's	where's	their	and
park	fixing	washing	she's	in	his	
restaurant	listening					

Everybody is busy today. Ms. Roberts is in the ___restaurant___ 1. She's _____ 2

dinner. Mr. and Mrs. Lopez are _____ 3 the health club. _____ 4 doing _____ 5

exercises. Patty and Danny Williams are in the _____ 6. She's _____ 7 the

newspaper. He's _____ 8 to music. Mr. _____ 9 Mrs. Sharp are also in the park.

What are they _____ 10? They're _____ 11 cards.

Jenny Chang is in the _____ 12. _____ 13 washing _____ 14 clothes.

Charlie Harris and Julie Carter _____ 15 in the parking lot. He's _____ 16

_____ 17 car. She's _____ 18 her bicycle. _____ 19 Mr. Molina? He's in the

_____ 20. _____ 21 he doing? _____ 22 reading a book.

MATCHING OPPOSITES

_d_	1. large	**a.** thin		___	8. tall	**h.** heavy
___	2. heavy	**b.** rich		___	9. difficult	**i.** old
___	3. single	**c.** beautiful		___	10. new	**j.** ugly
___	4. ugly	**d.** small		___	11. handsome	**k.** big
___	5. cheap	**e.** young		___	12. thin	**l.** easy
___	6. poor	**f.** expensive		___	13. little	**m.** noisy
___	7. old	**g.** married		___	14. quiet	**n.** short

B **WHAT ARE THEY SAYING?**

Tell me about your new friend.

1. Is he short or _____tall_____?

2. Is he heavy or _____?

3. Is he old or _____?

4. Is he single or _____?

Tell me about the apartment.

5. Is it large or _____?

6. Is it quiet or _____?

7. Is it cheap or _____?

8. Is it beautiful or _____?

C **LISTENING**

Listen and circle the word you hear.

1. small   (tall)   3. easy   noisy   5. ugly   young

2. ugly   heavy   4. thin   single   6. cheap   easy

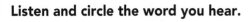

Activity Workbook   **27**

D WHAT'S WRONG?

| He She It } isn't | They aren't |

1. It's new.

_____It isn't new.____

_____It's old.____

2. They're quiet.

_____

_____

3. It's large.

_____

_____

4. He's single.

_____

_____

5. She's young.

_____

_____

6. They're short.

_____

_____

E SCRAMBLED QUESTIONS

Unscramble the questions. Begin each question with a capital letter.

1. _____Are you busy_____?
   busy   you   are

2. _____?
   dog   your   large   is

3. _____?
   they   are   married

4. _____?
   I   beautiful   am

5. _____?
   difficult   English   is

6. _____?
   new   is   car   their

7. _____?
   tall   she   is   short   or

8. _____?
   noisy   quiet   he   is   or

GRAMMARRAP: *Old! Cold! Tall! Small!*

Listen. Then clap and practice.

All.	Is he	young?	(clap) (clap)
	Is he	old?	(clap) (clap)
	Is it	hot?	(clap) (clap)
	Is it	cold?	(clap) (clap)
	Is she	short?	(clap) (clap)
	Is she	tall?	(clap) (clap)
	Is it	large?	(clap) (clap)
	Is it	small?	(clap) (clap)

Young!   Old!

Hot!   Cold!

Young!   Old!

Hot!   Cold!

A. Is he young or   old?

B.   He's very   old.

A.   Is it hot or   cold?

B.   It's very   cold.

A. Is she short or   tall?

B.   She's very   tall.

A.   Is it large or   small?

B.   It's extremely   small.

All.   Young!   Old!

Hot!   Cold!

Short!   Tall!

Large!   Small!

bicycle	book	car	cat	computer	dog	guitar	house	piano	TV

Albert

1. _____Albert's_____ _____car_____

Jenny

2. _____

George

3. _____

Fred

4. _____

Kate

5. _____

Mr. Price

6. _____

Jane

7. _____

Mike

8. _____

Mrs. Chang

9. _____

Alice

10. _____

WHAT'S THE WORD?

His	Her	Their	Its

1. Mary's brother isn't short.   (His (Her)) brother is tall.

2. Mr. and Mrs. Miller's apartment isn't cheap.   (His   Their) apartment is expensive.

3. Robert's sister isn't single.   (His   Her) sister is married.

4. Ms. Clark's neighbors aren't quiet.   (Their   Her) neighbors are noisy.

5. Their dog's name isn't Rover.   (Its   Their) name is Fido.

6. Mrs. Hunter's car isn't large.   (His   Her) car is small.

7. Timmy's bicycle isn't new.   (His   Its) bicycle is old.

8. Mr. and Mrs. Lee's son isn't single.   (Her   Their) son is married.

I **MR. AND MRS. GRANT**

Read the story and answer the questions.

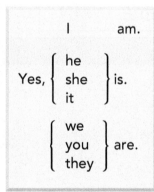

Meet Mr. and Mrs. Grant. Mr. Grant is short and heavy. Mrs. Grant is tall and thin. Their house is small and old. Their car is new and expensive. Their neighbors are noisy. And their cat is ugly.

1. Is Mr. Grant short? ____Yes, he is.____   8. Is their house large? _____

2. Is he tall? _____   9. Is it old? _____

3. Is he thin? _____   10. Is their car new? _____

4. Is he heavy? _____   11. Is it cheap? _____

5. Is Mrs. Grant tall? _____   12. Are their neighbors quiet? _____

6. Is she heavy? _____   13. Are they noisy? _____

7. Is she thin? _____   14. Is their cat pretty? _____

J HOW'S THE WEATHER?

it's sunny	it's raining	it's warm	it's hot
it's cloudy	it's snowing	it's cool	it's cold

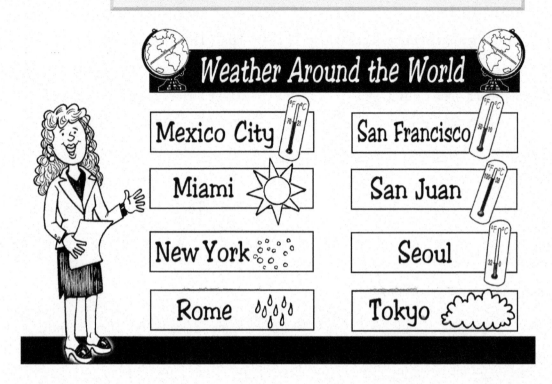

Weather Around the World

Mexico City
Miami
New York
Rome
San Francisco
San Juan
Seoul
Tokyo

1. How's the weather in Mexico City?   It's _____ warm. _____

2. How's the weather in Miami?   _____ _____

3. How's the weather in New York?   _____ _____

4. How's the weather in Rome?   _____ _____

5. How's the weather in San Francisco?   _____ _____

6. How's the weather in San Juan?   _____ _____

7. How's the weather in Seoul?   _____ _____

8. How's the weather in Tokyo?   _____ _____

9. How's the weather in YOUR city?   ....

K LISTENING

Listen and circle the word you hear.

1. cold   (cool)   3. sunny   snowing   5. raining   snowing

2. snowing   sunny   4. cool   hot   6. sunny   cloudy

Numbers

0	zero	10	ten	20	twenty	30	thirty
1	one	11	eleven	21	twenty-one	40	forty
2	two	12	twelve	22	twenty-two	50	fifty
3	three	13	thirteen	23	twenty-three	60	sixty
4	four	14	fourteen	24	twenty-four	70	seventy
5	five	15	fifteen	25	twenty-five	80	eighty
6	six	16	sixteen	26	twenty-six	90	ninety
7	seven	17	seventeen	27	twenty-seven	100	one hundred
8	eight	18	eighteen	28	twenty-eight		
9	nine	19	nineteen	29	twenty-nine		

L WHAT'S THE NUMBER?

1. twenty-four _____24_____
2. thirty-one _____
3. seventy-two _____
4. forty-six _____
5. ninety-seven _____

M WHAT'S THE WORD?

38 _____thirty-eight_____
83 _____
55 _____
99 _____
64 _____

N NUMBER PUZZLE

Across

2. 46
5. 29
8. 8
9. 0
10. 11
11. 50

Down

1. 60
3. 15
4. 7
5. 20
6. 12
7. 90

LISTENING

Listen to the temperature in Fahrenheit and Celsius. Write the numbers you hear.

1. Los Angeles _____86°_____ F/ _____30°_____ C   5. Miami _____ F/ _____ C

2. Seoul _____ F/ _____ C   6. London _____ F/ _____ C

3. San Juan _____ F/ _____ C   7. Mexico City _____ F/ _____ C

4. Hong Kong _____ F/ _____ C   8. Moscow _____ F/ _____ C

P **GRAMMARRAP:** *Terrible Weather! Beautiful Weather!*

Listen. Then clap and practice.

It's raining in	Alaska.
It's snowing in	L.A.
It's cloudy in	Caracas.
It's TERRIBLE	today!
It's warm in	Pennsylvania.
It's sunny in	Bombay.
It's cool in	Guatemala.
It's BEAUTIFUL	today!

Q **MATCHING**

Match the questions and answers.

_e_ 1. Is your brother tall?   a. Yes, I am. I'm studying.

____ 2. Is your computer new?   b. No, she isn't. She's single.

____ 3. Is it hot today?   c. No, she isn't. She's old.

____ 4. Hi! Are you busy?   d. No, it isn't. It's cold.

____ 5. Are your neighbors quiet?   e. No, he isn't. He's short.

____ 6. Is she young?   f. No, he isn't. He's thin.

____ 7. Is her husband heavy?   g. No, they aren't. They're easy.

____ 8. Is your sister married?   h. No, it isn't. It's old.

____ 9. Are these questions difficult?   i. No, they aren't. They're noisy.

brother	sister
children	son
daughter	wife
husband	

father	grandmother
grandchildren	grandparents
granddaughter	grandson
grandfather	mother

Bill and Jane are married. Jane is Bill's _____wife_____ 1. Bill is Jane's _____ 2.

Timmy and Sally are their _____ 3. Timmy is their _____ 4, and Sally is their

_____ 5. Timmy is Sally's _____ 6, and Sally is Timmy's _____ 7.

Walter and Helen are Jane's parents. Walter is Jane's _____ 8, and Helen is Jane's

_____ 9. Walter and Helen are Timmy and Sally's _____ 10. Walter is

their _____ 11, and Helen is their _____ 12. Timmy and Sally are

Walter and Helen's _____ 13. Timmy is their _____ 14, and Sally

is their _____ 15.

aunt	nephew	uncle
cousin	niece	

John is Jane's brother. Judy is John's wife.

Danny is their son. John is Timmy and Sally's

_____ 16, and Judy is their _____ 17.

Timmy is John and Judy's _____ 18,

and Sally is their _____ 19. Danny is

Timmy and Sally's _____ 20.

Listen and put a check (✓) under the correct picture.

1. _____✓_____   _____   2. _____   _____

3. _____   _____   4. _____   _____

5. _____   _____   6. _____   _____

7. _____   _____   8. _____   _____

C THE WRONG WORD!

Put a circle around the wrong word.

1.	large	small	(cheap)	little	6.	rugs	parents	cousins	children
2.	kitchen	bathroom	bedroom	park	7.	pencil	book	pen	bank
3.	guitar	baseball	drums	piano	8.	Miss	Mr.	Ms.	Mrs.
4.	handsome	beautiful	tall	pretty	9.	quiet	noisy	poor	loud
5.	hot	dinner	warm	cool	10.	son	sister	nephew	brother

D GRAMMARSONG: *Pictures on the Wall*

Listen and fill in the words to the song. Then listen again and sing along.

crying	dancing	hanging	having	living	looking	smiling	working

I'm looking at the photographs.

They're hanging in the hall.

I'm ____smiling____ ¹ at the memories,

looking at the pictures on the wall.

My son Robert's married now.

I'm _____ ² in L.A. (Hi, Dad!)

My daughter's _____ ³ in Detroit.

I'm very far away. (I love you, Dad!)

I'm _____ ⁴ at the photographs.

They're _____ ⁵ in the hall.

I'm smiling at the memories,

looking at the pictures on the wall.

My mom and dad are _____ ⁶.

It's a very special day.

(We're _____ ⁷ a good time!)

My little sister's _____ ⁸.

It's my brother's wedding day.
(I'm so happy!)

I'm _____ ⁹ at the photographs.

They're _____ ¹⁰ in the hall.

I'm _____ ¹¹ at the memories,

_____ ¹² at the pictures on the wall.

I'm smiling at the memories,

looking at the pictures on the wall.

E AN E-MAIL FROM LOS ANGELES

```
To: alex@ttm.com
From: bob@aal.com

Dear Alex,

    Our new home in Los Angeles is large and pretty. Los Angeles is
beautiful. The weather is warm and sunny. Today it's 78°F.
    Our family is in the park today, and we're having a good time. My
mother is reading a book, and my father is listening to music. My sister
Patty is riding her bicycle, and my brother Tom is skateboarding.
    My grandparents aren't in the park today. They're at home. My
grandmother is baking, and my grandfather is planting flowers
in the yard.
    How's the weather in New York today? Is it snowing? What are
you and your family doing?
```

Answer these questions in complete sentences.

1. Where is Bob's new home? _____ It's in Los Angeles. _____

2. How's the weather in Los Angeles? _____

3. What's the temperature? _____

4. Where are Bob and his family today? _____

5. What's Bob's mother doing? _____

6. What's his father doing? _____

7. Who is Patty? _____

8. What's she doing? _____

9. Who is Tom? _____

10. What's he doing? _____

11. Are Bob's grandparents in the park? _____

12. Where are they? _____

13. What's his grandmother doing? _____

14. What's his grandfather doing? _____

15. Is Alex in Los Angeles? _____

16. Where is he? _____

F **GrammarRap:** *No. She's in Spain.*

Listen. Then clap and practice.

A.   What's Jack   doing?

B.   He's working in   Rome.

A. What's BOB   doing?

B.   He's working at   HOME.

A.   Is Jack at   home?

B.   No. HE'S in   ROME.

A.   Is BOB in   Rome?

B.   No. HE'S at   HOME.

All.   Jack's in   Rome.

              Jack's in   Rome.

     What's BOB   doing?

       He's working at   HOME.

A.   What's Jane   doing?

B.   She's working in Spain.

A. What's MARY   doing?

B.   She's working in MAINE.

A.   Is Jane in   Maine?

B.   No. SHE'S in   SPAIN.

A.   Is Mary in   Spain?

B.   No. SHE'S in   MAINE.

All.   Jane's in   Spain.

              Jane's in   Spain.

     What's MARY   doing?

     She's working in   MAINE.

✔ **CHECK-UP TEST: Chapters 4–6**

A. Circle the correct answers.

Ex. Jack is sitting on his
computer
TV
(bicycle)

1. He's my
nephew
wife
sister

2. We're standing
on
at
in
front of our house.

3. They're swimming at the
yard
kitchen
beach

4. He's feeding the dog
its
it's
he
dinner.

5. He's sleeping
at
on
in
the sofa.

6. Mrs. Kent is
raining
feeding
reading
in the park.

7. We're
fixing
snowing
riding
our car.

8. They're
painting
eating
brushing
their teeth.

B. Fill in the blanks.

Ex. ___What's___ his name?

1. _____ are they? They're in Tahiti.

2. My mother's mother is my _____.

3. My sister's daughter is my _____.

4. _____ is he? He's my cousin.

5. Mr. Jones is playing a game on _____ computer.

6. My children are doing _____ homework.

7. Ms. Kim is busy. She's fixing _____ sink.

C. Write a sentence with the opposite adjective.

Ex. Their car isn't cheap. ___It's expensive.___

1. My brother isn't heavy. _____

2. They aren't short. _____

3. My computer isn't old. _____

D. Write the question.

Ex. ___Is it ugly?___ No, it isn't. It's beautiful.

1. _____ No, I'm not. I'm single.

2. _____ No, she isn't. She's old.

3. _____ No, they aren't. They're noisy.

E. Listen and choose the correct response.

Ex. No, he isn't. (a.) He's young. b. He's thin.

1. No, it isn't. a. It's difficult. b. It's small.

2. No, she isn't. a. She's rich. b. She's short.

3. No, it isn't. a. It's easy. b. It's cloudy.

4. No, he isn't. a. He's tall. b. He's loud.

A A FAMILY TREE

Look at the diagram on student book page 53 and answer the questions.

1. Who are Sally's parents?
   a. Jimmy and Sarah
   b. Julie and Kevin
   c. Patty and Tom
   d. Betty and Henry

2. Who is single?
   a. Jack
   b. Linda
   c. Patty
   d. Tom

3. Who is Sally and Jack's son?
   a. Henry
   b. Sarah
   c. Jimmy
   d. Kevin

4. Who is Tom's wife?
   a. Patty
   b. Linda
   c. Sally
   d. Julie

5. Who is Kevin's uncle?
   a. Tom
   b. Jack
   c. Jimmy
   d. Henry

6. Who are Sarah's cousins?
   a. Patty and Tom
   b. Julie and Jimmy
   c. Julie and Kevin
   d. Patty and Linda

7. Who is Patty and Tom's nephew?
   a. Jimmy
   b. Sarah
   c. Jack
   d. Sally

8. Who are Betty's grandchildren?
   a. Sally and Jack
   b. Patty and Tom
   c. Jimmy and Julie
   d. Sally, Linda, and Tom

9. Who is Sally and Jack's niece?
   a. Sarah
   b. Julie
   c. Linda
   d. Patty

10. Who is Julie's aunt?
    a. Betty
    b. Patty
    c. Sarah
    d. Linda

SIDE by SIDE Gazette

STUDENT BOOK
PAGES 53–54

B BUILD YOUR VOCABULARY! What's the Word?

Choose the correct word.

1. She's [erasing / (opening)] her book.

2. I'm [writing / using] a calculator.

3. He's closing his [book / board].

4. The student is [raising / writing] her name.

5. I'm [reading / riding] a book.

6. The teacher is [vacuuming / erasing] the board.

7. He's [erasing / raising] his hand.

8. I'm [opening / closing] my book, and I'm reading the question.

BUILD YOUR VOCABULARY! True or False?

Look at the picture of a classroom on student book page 8. Answer True (T) or False (F).

_F_ 1. The teacher is erasing the board.

____ 2. The student on the right is opening her book.

____ 3. One student is using a calculator.

____ 4. One student is writing with a pencil.

____ 5. The teacher is reading a book.

____ 6. The teacher is writing with chalk.

____ 7. One student is raising her hand.

____ 8. One student is writing with a pen.

D FACT FILE

Look at the Fact File on student book page 54. Write the correct word to complete the conversation.

1. A. Is he your father-in-law?

   B. Yes. He's my wife's _____father_____.

2. A. Is this your husband's mother?

   B. Yes. She's my _____.

3. A. Is he your daughter's _____?

   B. Yes. He's my son-in-law.

4. A. Is this your son's wife?

   B. Yes. She's my _____.

5. A. Is he your wife's brother?

   B. Yes. He's my _____.

6. A. Is this your daughter's husband?

   B. Yes. He's my _____.

7. A. Is she your husband's _____?

   B. Yes. She's my sister-in-law.

8. A. Is she your son's _____?

   B. Yes. She's my daughter-in-law.

E "CAN-DO" REVIEW

Match the "can do" statement and the correct sentence.

_c_ 1. I can ask about current activities.

____ 2. I can tell about my daily activities.

____ 3. I can ask a person's location.

____ 4. I can describe people.

____ 5. I can describe objects.

____ 6. I can describe the weather.

____ 7. I can call someone on the telephone.

____ 8. I can identify my family members.

____ 9. I can introduce people.

____ 10. I can describe a person's emotions.

a. His car is old.

b. I'd like to introduce my father.

c. What are you doing?

d. Hello. Is this Evelyn?

e. Where's your brother?

f. He's my son.

g. I'm washing my clothes.

h. It's sunny.

i. She's very happy.

j. He's short.

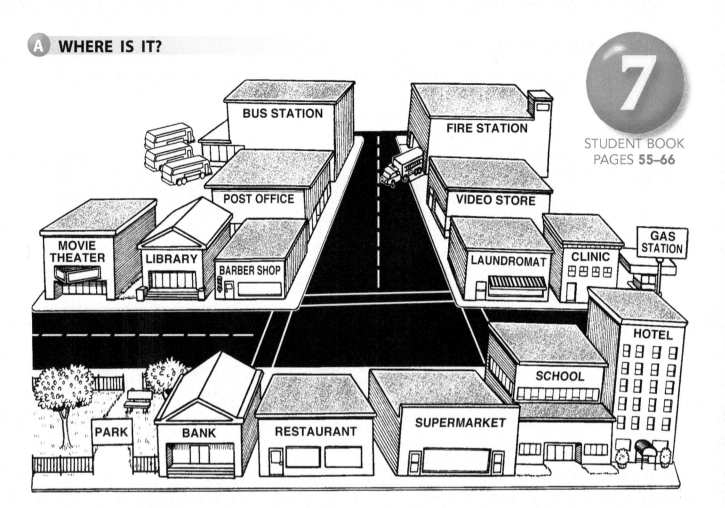

| across from | around the corner from | next to | between |

1. The bank is _____next to_____ the restaurant.

2. The bus station is _____ the fire station.

3. The library is _____ the movie theater and the barber shop.

4. The laundromat is _____ the video store.

5. The laundromat is _____ the clinic.

6. The clinic is _____ the laundromat and the gas station.

7. The clinic and the gas station are _____ the hotel.

8. The barber shop is _____ the post office.

9. The restaurant is _____ the supermarket.

10. The school is _____ the supermarket and the hotel.

11. The school is _____ the laundromat.

Is there	There's	across from	around the corner from
there		between	next to

1. Excuse me. Is there a bank in this neighborhood?

   Yes, there is. ___There's___ a bank on Park Street, ___next to___ the school.

2. Excuse me. _____ a video store in this neighborhood?

   Yes, there is. _____ a video store on Main Street, _____ the clinic.

3. Excuse me. Is there a supermarket in this neighborhood?

   Yes, _____ is. _____ a supermarket on School Street, _____ the post office.

4. Excuse me. _____ a park in this neighborhood?

   Yes, there is. _____ a park on State Street, _____ the drug store and the library.

5. Excuse me. _____ a gas station in this neighborhood?

   Yes, _____ is. _____ a gas station on _____ Avenue, _____ the fire station.

C LISTENING

Listen to the sentences about the buildings on the map. After each sentence, write the name on the correct building.

1.	bakery	4.	library	7.	hair salon	10.	park
2.	school	5.	hospital	8.	supermarket	11.	health club
3.	department store	6.	police station	9.	video store	12.	train station

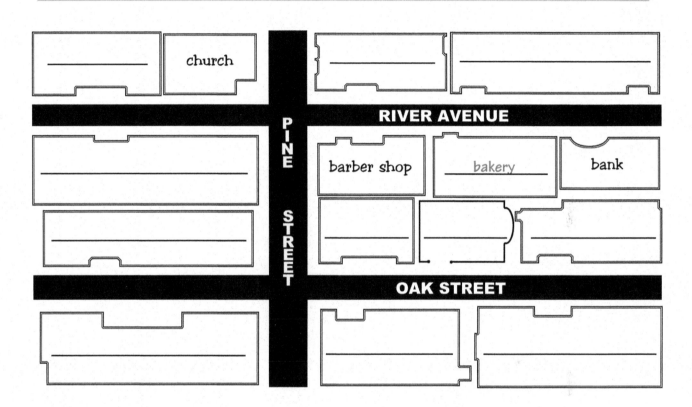

D YES OR NO?

Look at the map and answer the questions.

1. Is there a fire station on Oak Street?   Yes, there is.   No, there isn't.

2. Is there a hair salon across from the barber shop?   Yes, there is.   No, there isn't.

3. Is there a supermarket around the corner from the bank?   Yes, there is.   No, there isn't.

4. Is there a police station next to the hospital?   Yes, there is.   No, there isn't.

5. Is there a department store across from the school?   Yes, there is.   No, there isn't.

6. Is there a drug store on Oak Street?   Yes, there is.   No, there isn't.

7. Is there a laundromat next to the park?   Yes, there is.   No, there isn't.

8. Is there a church on River Avenue?   Yes, there is.   No, there isn't.

9. Is there a bank between the barber shop and the bakery?   Yes, there is.   No, there isn't.

Activity Workbook   **43**

E GRAMMARRAP: *Just Around the Corner*

Listen. Then clap and practice.

All.	There's a nice big	supermarket	just around the	corner.
	There's a good cheap	restaurant	just around the	corner.
	There's a nice clean	laundromat	just around the	corner.
	There's a quiet little	park	just around the	corner.
	Just around the	corner?	Thanks	very much.

A.	Is there a nice big	supermarket	anywhere	around here?
B.	Yes, there	is.	Yes, there	is.
	There's a nice big	supermarket	just around the	corner.
A.	Just around the	corner?	Thanks very	much.

A.	Is there a good cheap	restaurant	anywhere	around here?
B.	Yes, there	is.	Yes, there	is.
	There's a good cheap	restaurant	just around the	corner.
A.	Just around the	corner?	Thanks very	much.

A.	Is there a nice clean	laundromat	anywhere	around here?
B.	Yes, there	is.	Yes, there	is.
	There's a nice clean	laundromat	just around the	corner.
A.	Just around the	corner?	Thanks very	much.

A.	Is there a quiet little	park	anywhere	around here?
B.	Yes, there	is.	Yes, there	is.
	There's a quiet little	park	just around the	corner.
A.	Just around the	corner?	Thanks very	much.

F WHAT ARE THEY SAYING?

is there	there is	there isn't	there are
are there	there's		there aren't

1. ___Is___ ___there___ an elevator in the building?

2. Yes, _____ _____.

3. How many closets _____ _____ in the apartment?

4. _____ a large closet in the bedroom, and _____ _____ two small closets in the living room.

5. _____ _____ a jacuzzi in the bathroom?

6. No, _____ _____. But _____ _____ two air conditioners in the apartment.

7. _____ _____ any washing machines in the building?

8. No, _____ _____. But _____ a laundromat across the street.

9. How many windows _____ _____ in the apartment?

10. _____ _____ three windows in the living room, and _____ one window in the bedroom.

G OUR APARTMENT BUILDING

broken	closets	escape	machines	satellite dish	mice
cats	dogs	hole	mailbox	refrigerator	stop

1. There aren't any washing _____machines_____ in the basement.

2. There's a _____ window in the bathroom.

3. There are _____ in the basement.

4. There isn't a fire _____.

5. There's a _____ in the wall in the living room.

6. There's a _____ on the roof.

7. There's a _____ in the kitchen.

8. There are two _____ in the bedroom.

9. There aren't any _____ in the building, but there are _____.

10. There isn't a bus _____ outside the building, but there's a _____.

H JANE'S LIVING ROOM

Yes, there is. No, there isn't.	Yes, there are. No, there aren't.

1. Is there a computer in Jane's living room?

   _____ Yes, there is. _____

2. Is there a desk in the living room?

   _____

3. Are there any flowers in the living room?

   _____

4. Is there a newspaper on the table?

   _____

5. Are there any photographs on the table?

   _____

6. Are there any clothes in the closet?

   _____

7. Are there any windows in the living room?

   _____

8. Is there a cat in the living room?

   _____

9. Are there any chairs in front of the windows?

   _____

10. Is there a bookshelf in the living room?

    _____

11. Is there a cell phone next to the computer?

    _____

12. Is there a television next to the bookshelf?

    _____

13. Are there any books on the sofa?

    _____

14. Is there a guitar on the chair?

    _____

1 LOOKING FOR AN APARTMENT

a/c. = air conditioner	beaut. = beautiful	frpl(s). = fireplace(s)	nr. = near
apt. = apartment	bldg. = building	kit. = kitchen	rm(s). = room(s)
bath(s). = bathroom(s)	dinrm. = dining room	lge. = large	schl. = school
bdrm(s). = bedroom(s)	elev. = elevator	livrm. = living room	

www.UShomes.com   **CHICAGO**

Quiet, sunny apt., kit., livrm., bdrm., bath., 2 frpls., no children, $900. 800-874-5555.

1. The apartment is in ____Chicago____.

2. It's quiet and _____.

3. There's a kitchen, a living room, a _____, and a _____.

4. There are two _____ in the apartment.

5. There aren't any _____ in the building.

www.UShomes.com   **MIAMI**

Beaut. new apt., kit., livrm., 3 bdrms., 2 baths., elev. in building., $1200. 800-874-5555.

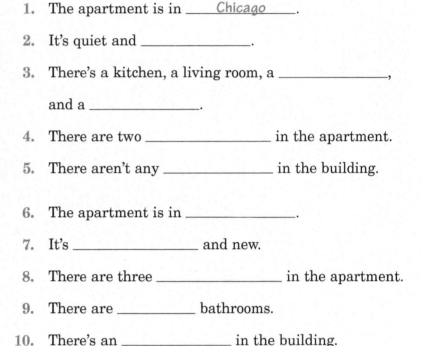

6. The apartment is in _____.

7. It's _____ and new.

8. There are three _____ in the apartment.

9. There are _____ bathrooms.

10. There's an _____ in the building.

www.UShomes.com   **NEW YORK**

Sunny, lge. apt., kit., livrm., bdrm., bath., 2 a/c., nr. schl. $1800. 800-874-5555.

11. The apartment is in _____.

12. It's sunny and _____.

13. There's a kitchen, a _____, a bedroom, and a bathroom.

14. There are two _____.

15. The apartment is near a _____.

www.UShomes.com   **DALLAS**

Lge. quiet apt., kit., livrm., dinrm., 2 bdrms., 2 baths., elev. in bldg., nr. bus. $850. 800-874-5555.

16. The apartment is in _____.

17. It's large and _____.

18. There's a _____, a kitchen, and a living room.

19. There's an elevator in the _____.

20. The apartment is _____ a bus stop.

48   Activity Workbook

Listen. Then clap and practice.

There are

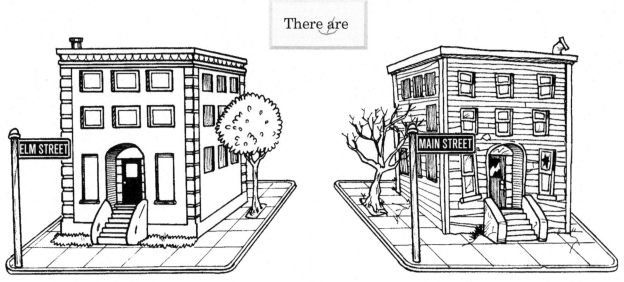

A.   Tell me about the apartment on   Elm Street.

B.   It's nice, but it   isn't very   cheap.

    There's a brand new   stove in the   kitchen.

    There's a beautiful   carpet on the   floor.

    There are three large   windows in the   living room.

    And the bedroom has a   sliding glass   door.

All.   The bedroom has a   sliding glass   door?!

B.   Yes, the bedroom has a   sliding glass   door.

A.   Tell me about the apartment on   Main Street.

B.   It's cheap, but it   isn't very   nice.

    There isn't a   tub in the   bathroom.

    There aren't any   lights in the   hall.

    There's a broken   window in the   dining room.

    And there are ten big   holes in the   wall!

All.   There are ten big   holes in the   wall?!

B.   Yes, there are ten big   holes in the   wall.

belt	briefcase	glasses	jeans	purse	sock	tie
blouse	coat	glove	mitten	shirt	stocking	umbrella
boots	dress	hat	necklace	shoe	suit	watch
bracelet	earring	jacket	pants	skirt	sweater	

STUDENT BOOK
PAGES 67–76

1. _____tie_____   6. _____   11. _____

2. _____   7. _____   12. _____

3. _____   8. _____   13. _____

4. _____   9. _____   14. _____

5. _____   10. _____   15. _____

16. _____   20. _____   24. _____

17. _____   21. _____   25. _____

18. _____   22. _____   26. _____

19. _____   23. _____   27. _____

B A OR AN?

1. __a__ bus station
2. __an__ umbrella
3. _____ school
4. _____ office
5. _____ radio
6. _____ earring

7. _____ hospital
8. _____ antenna
9. _____ e-mail
10. _____ yard
11. _____ library
12. _____ cell phone

13. _____ exercise
14. _____ house
15. _____ bank
16. _____ woman
17. _____ apartment
18. _____ laundromat

19. _____ uncle
20. _____ attic
21. _____ flower
22. _____ aunt
23. _____ fax
24. _____ hotel

C SINGULAR/PLURAL

1. ____a hat____   hats
2. _____   basements
3. a dress   _____
4. a boss   _____
5. an exercise   _____
6. _____   watches
7. _____   gloves
8. a sock   _____
9. a drum   _____

10. _____   rooms
11. an earring   _____
12. _____   purses
13. a niece   _____
14. a woman   _____
15. _____   children
16. a mouse   _____
17. _____   teeth
18. _____   people

D LISTENING

Listen and circle the word you hear.

1. umbrella   (umbrellas)
2. blouse   blouses
3. coat   coats
4. computer   computers
5. shoe   shoes
6. exercise   exercises
7. dress   dresses
8. restaurant   restaurants

9. necklace   necklaces
10. earring   earrings
11. belt   belts
12. watch   watches
13. niece   nieces
14. nephew   nephews
15. shirt   shirts
16. tie   ties

E LISTENING 🔊

Listen and circle the color you hear.

1. (blue)   black   3. gray   gold   5. purple   yellow

2. red   green   4. pink   silver   6. orange   brown

F COLORS

Write sentences about yourself, using colors.

black	gray	pink	silver
blue	green	purple	white
brown	orange	red	yellow
gold			

1. My house/apartment is ....

2. My bedroom is ....

3. My kitchen is ....

4. My bathroom is ....

5. My living room is ....

6. My classroom is ....

7. My English book is ....

8. My pencils are ....

9. My notebook is ....

10. My desk is ....

11. My shirt/blouse is ....

12. My watch is ....

13. My socks/stockings are ....

14. My coat is ....

15. My hat is ....

16. My jeans are ....

17. My shoes are ....

18. My .... (is/are) ....

19. My .... (is/are) ....

20. My .... (is/are) ....

21. My .... (is/are) ....

22. My .... (is/are) ....

23. My .... (is/are) ....

24. My .... (is/are) ....

1. Yes, please. I'm looking for

_____ a pair of pants _____ .

2. Yes, please. I'm looking for

_____ .

3. Yes, please. I'm looking for

_____ .

4. Yes, please. I'm looking for

_____ .

5. Yes, please. I'm looking for

_____ .

6. Yes, please. I'm looking for

_____ .

7. Yes, please. I'm looking for

_____ .

8. Yes, please. I'm looking for

_____ .

9. Yes, please. I'm looking for

_____ .

H LISTENING

Listen and put a check (✓) under the correct picture.

1. _____   ✓ _____   2. _____

3. _____   _____   4. _____   _____

5. _____   _____   6. _____   _____

7. _____   _____   8. _____   _____

I LISTENING

Listen and circle the correct word to complete the sentence.

1. (is) / are red.   4. is / are gold.   7. is / are expensive.

2. is / are easy.   5. is / are beautiful.   8. is / are small.

3. is / are large.   6. is / are new.   9. is / are big.

54   Activity Workbook

J THIS /THAT /THESE /THOSE

 this / these

that / those

  orange

  yellow

1. _____This hat is orange._____

2. _____That hat is yellow._____

  brown

  black

3. _____

4. _____

  expensive

  cheap

5. _____

6. _____

  small

  large

7. _____

8. _____

  pretty

ugly

9. _____

10. _____

  gold

 silver

11. _____

12. _____

K SINGULAR → PLURAL

Write the sentence in the plural.

1. That coat is blue.   _Those coats are blue._

2. This bracelet is new.   _____

3. That watch is beautiful.   _____

4. This is Tom's jacket.   _____

5. This isn't your shoe.   _____

6. Is that your earring?   _____

7. That isn't your notebook.   _____

8. This person isn't rich.   _____

L PLURAL → SINGULAR

Write the sentence in the singular.

1. These sweaters are pretty.   _This sweater is pretty._

2. Those purses are expensive.   _____

3. Are these your neighbors?   _____

4. Are those your dresses?   _____

5. Those are Bill's shirts.   _____

6. These women are my friends.   _____

7. These aren't my gloves.   _____

8. Those are her cats.   _____

M SCRAMBLED SENTENCES

Unscramble the sentences. Begin each sentence with a capital letter.

1. _____I think that's my jacket._____   4. _____
   jacket I that's think my   year blue very this suits popular are

2. _____   5. _____
   my these gloves new are   of here's nice sunglasses pair a

3. _____   6. _____
   boots aren't those black your   old that's car brother's my

N GRAMMARRAP: *Clothes In My Closet*

Listen. Then clap and practice.

This shirt is	red.		Old	red	shirt!
That skirt is	blue.		New	blue	skirt!
This shirt is	old.		Old	red	shirt!
That skirt is	new.		New	blue	skirt!

These suits are	silver.		New	silver	suits!
Those boots are	gold.		Old	gold	boots!
These suits are	new.		New	silver	suits!
Those boots are	old.		Old	gold	boots!

O GRAMMARRAP: *Black Leather Jacket*

Listen. Then clap and practice.

Blue	jeans,	gray	pants,
Black	leather	jacket!	
Blue	jeans,	gray	pants,
Black	leather	jacket!	

White	shirt,	silver	boots,
Black	leather	jacket!	
White	shirt,	silver	boots,
Black	leather	jacket!	

Cool	blue	jeans!	
Nice	gray	pants!	
White	shirt,	silver	boots,
Black	leather	jacket!	

Activity Workbook   **57**

P THIS/ THAT/ THESE/ THOSE

this	that
these	those

1. _____This_____ is my favorite pair of jeans.

_____ are my new sweaters, and

_____ is my new coat.

2. _____That_____ 's a pretty coat.

Are _____ your new boots?

3. _____ is my classroom.

_____ is the bulletin board, and

_____ are the computers.

4. Are _____ your books, and

is _____ your pencil?

5. _____ is my favorite photograph.

_____ is my mother, and

_____ are my sisters and brothers.

6. Are _____ your cousins?

Who's _____ handsome man?

Q GRAMMARSONG: *At the Laundromat*

Listen and fill in the words to the song. Then listen again and sing along.

hat	those	shirt	suits	that	are	skirt	that's	boots	these	this

Is ___this___ [1] your sweater?

Is _____ [2] your _____ [3]?

_____ [4] my blue jacket.

That's my pink _____ [5].

I think _____ [6] is my new _____ [7].

We're looking for _____ [8] and _____ [9].

We're washing all our clothes at the laundromat.

_____ [10] and that. At the laundromat.

This and _____ [11]. At the laundromat.

_____ [12] and _____ [13]. At the laundromat.

Are _____ [14] your mittens?

_____ [15] these your _____ [16]?

_____ [17] are my socks.

Those are my bathing _____ [18].

Where _____ [19] my pantyhose?

We're looking for _____ [20] and _____ [21].

We're washing all our clothes at the laundromat.

_____ [22] and _____ [23].

Washing all our clothes.

_____ [24] and _____ [25].

At the laundromat. At the laundromat.

(Hey! Give me _____ [26]!)

At the laundromat!

✔ CHECK-UP TEST: Chapters 7–8

A. Circle the correct answers.

Ex. My favorite color is [broken / (blue) / big].

1. Are [these / this / that] your children?

2. Here's a nice pair [to / on / of] stockings.

3. [Are there / Is there / There] a jacuzzi in the apartment?

4. There's an [earring / sweater / umbrellas] on the table.

5. [Who / What / How] many windows are there in the living room?

6. There aren't any [man / people / hole] in the room.

7. Dresses are over [there / their / they're].

8. Is there a stove in the kitchen?

No, there aren't.
No, they isn't.
No, there isn't.

B. Answer the questions.

Ex. Where's the book store?

It's next to the bank.

1. Where's the bakery?

_____

2. Where's the hospital?

_____

3. Where's the video store?

_____

C. **Circle the word that doesn't belong.**

Ex. cotton   wool   vinyl   (cheap)

1. this   those   their   these

2. orange   striped   gray   pink

3. closet   bakery   hotel   school

4. boots   necklace   shoes   socks

D. **Write sentences with *this*, *that*, *these*, and *those*.**

old

Ex. _____This car is old._____

large

1. _____

broken

2. _____

black

3. _____

E. **Write these sentences in the plural.**

Ex. That house is large.

    _____Those houses are large._____

1. This room is small.

_____

2. That isn't my pencil.

_____

3. Is this your boot?

_____

F. **Listen and circle the correct word to complete the sentence.**

Ex. 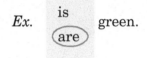 green.
    is
    (are)

1. is
    are   old.

2. is
    are   nice.

3. is
    are   beautiful.

4. is
    are   expensive.

A CLOTHING, COLORS, AND CULTURES

Read the article on student book page 77 and answer the questions.

1. _____ is a common clothing color for little boys in many cultures.
   a. Red
   b. White
   c. Blue
   d. Pink

2. White is the traditional color of a wedding _____ in many cultures.
   a. ring
   b. belt
   c. coat
   d. dress

3. There are different colors for special _____. St. Patrick's Day is a holiday when green is very popular.
   a. days
   b. places
   c. people
   d. stores

4. Wedding dresses in China are red because it's a _____ color.
   a. sad
   b. lucky
   c. quiet
   d. young

5. White is a _____.
   a. happy color in all cultures
   b. sad color in all cultures
   c. sad color in some cultures
   d. traditional wedding color in all cultures

6. The main topic of this article is _____.
   a. happy colors around the world
   b. sad colors around the world
   c. common clothing for children
   d. the meanings of colors in different cultures

SIDE by SIDE
Gazette
STUDENT BOOK
PAGES **77–78**

B BUILD YOUR VOCABULARY! Crossword

Across

3.

4.

5.

6.

7.

Down

1.

2.

5.

 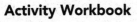

C FACT FILE: Urban, Suburban, and Rural

Look at the Fact File on student book page 78 and answer the questions.

1. Los Angeles and New York City are _____.
   a. urban areas
   b. suburban areas
   c. rural areas

2. Huts and farmhouses far from the city are in _____.
   a. urban areas
   b. suburban areas
   c. rural areas

3. Roberto is living in an apartment house on a busy street with many tall buildings. He's living in _____.
   a. an urban area
   b. a suburban area
   c. a rural area

4. Small towns near big cities are _____.
   a. urban areas
   b. suburban areas
   c. rural areas

5. About 50% of the people in the world are in _____.
   a. urban areas
   b. suburban areas
   c. rural areas

6. Marina is working in Chicago. Her house is on a quiet street twenty minutes outside the city in _____.
   a. an urban area
   b. a suburban area
   c. a rural area

D FACT FILE: Think About It

What are some reasons for living in a city, in a suburb, or in the countryside? What are some problems? Make a list of good things and bad things about urban, suburban, and rural areas.

	Urban Areas	Suburban Areas	Rural Areas
Good			
Bad			

E "CAN-DO" REVIEW

Match the "can do" statement and the correct sentence.

____ 1. I can ask the location of places.

____ 2. I can give the location of places.

____ 3. I can describe my home.

____ 4. I can ask about an apartment for rent.

____ 5. I can offer to help a customer.

____ 6. I can express gratitude.

____ 7. I can agree with someone.

____ 8. I can disagree with someone.

____ 9. I can compliment someone.

____ 10. I can apologize.

a. There's a small kitchen in my apartment.

b. I don't think so.

c. May I help you?

d. You're right.

e. I'm sorry.

f. Where's the library?

g. That's a very nice sweater.

h. Is there a closet in the bedroom?

i. Thank you.

j. The post office is next to the school.

STUDENT BOOK
PAGES **79–86**

what	language	we	our	is	eat	read
what's	name	you	your	are	live	watch
where	names	they	their	do	sing	speak

A. <u>What's</u> ¹ your name?

B. My _____ ² _____ ³ Sung Hee.

A. Where _____ ⁴ _____ ⁵ live?

B. I _____ ⁶ in Seoul.

A. _____ ⁷ _____ ⁸ do you speak?

B. I _____ ⁹ Korean.

A. What _____ ¹⁰ _____ ¹¹ do every day?

B. Every day I _____ ¹² Korean food, and

  I _____ ¹³ Korean TV shows.

A. What _____ ¹⁴ your names?

B. _____ ¹⁵ _____ ¹⁶ are Carlos and Maria.

A. Where _____ ¹⁷ _____ ¹⁸ live?

B. _____ ¹⁹ _____ ²⁰ in Madrid.

A. _____ ²¹ language _____ ²² _____ ²³ speak?

B. We _____ ²⁴ Spanish.

A. What _____ ²⁵ you _____ ²⁶ every day?

B. Every day _____ ²⁷ _____ ²⁸ Spanish songs,

  and we _____ ²⁹ Spanish newspapers.

A. _____ 30 _____ 31 their names?

B. _____ 32 _____ 33 _____ 34

Yuko and Toshi.

A. _____ 35 _____ 36 they live?

B. _____ 37 _____ 38 in Kyoto.

A. _____ 39 _____ 40 _____ 41

_____ 42 speak?

B. They _____ 43 Japanese.

A. What _____ 44 they _____ 45 every day?

B. Every day _____ 46 _____ 47 Japanese food,

and _____ 48 _____ 49 Japanese TV shows.

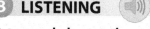 **LISTENING**

Listen and choose the correct response.

1. a. My name is Kenji.
   b. I live in Tokyo.

2. a. They speak Italian.
   b. I speak Italian.

3. a. They watch Russian TV shows.
   b. I watch Russian TV shows.

4. a. We live in Seoul.
   b. They live in Seoul.

5. a. We eat French food.
   b. We speak French.

6. a. They live in Madrid.
   b. We sing Spanish songs.

C **PEOPLE AROUND THE WORLD**

My name is Jane. I live in Montreal.
Every day I play the piano, and I
listen to Canadian music.

1. What's her name?   Her name is Jane.

2. Where does she live?   _____

3. What does she do every day?   _____

(continued)

Activity Workbook   **63**

My name is Omar. I live in Cairo. I speak Arabic. Every day I eat Egyptian food, and I read Egyptian newspapers.

4. _____? His name is Omar.

5. _____? He lives in Cairo.

6. What language does he speak? _____

7. What _____ every day? He _____ Egyptian food, and _____

_____.

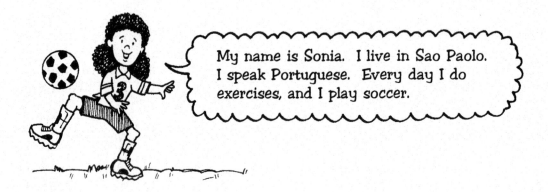

My name is Sonia. I live in Sao Paolo. I speak Portuguese. Every day I do exercises, and I play soccer.

8. What's her name? _____

9. _____ she live? _____

10. What language _____? _____

11. What _____ every day? _____

_____

D WRITE ABOUT YOURSELF

1. What's your name? ....

2. Where do you live? ....

3. What language do you speak? ....

4. What do you do every day? ....

....

E **GRAMMARRAP:** *People and Places*

Listen. Then clap and practice.

A. What's his name?

B. His name is Joe.

A. Where does he live?

B. In Mexico.

A. What's her name?

B. Her name is Anne.

A. Where does she live?

B. She lives in Japan.

A. What's her name?

B. Her name is Denise.

A. Where does she live?

B. She lives in Greece.

A. What's his name?

B. His name is Lance.

A. Where does he live?

B. He lives in France.

A. What's her name?

B. Her name is Anastasia.

A. Where does she live?

B. She lives in Malaysia.

A. What's her name?

B. Her name is Maria.

A. Where does she live?

B. She lives in Korea.

F EDUARDO'S FAMILY

Fill in the correct form of the verb.

clean	cook	do	live	play	read	shop	speak	work
cleans	cooks	does	lives	plays	reads	shops	speaks	works

My name is Eduardo. I _____live_____¹ in Rio de Janeiro. I _____² English and

Portuguese. My wife's name is Sonia. She _____³ English, Portuguese, and Spanish. Our

children, Fernando and Claudio, also _____⁴ English and Portuguese. At school they

_____⁵ English and Portuguese books.

We _____⁶ in a large apartment. Every day my wife _____⁷ the newspaper

and _____⁸ in a bank. I _____⁹ breakfast and _____¹⁰ in an office.

Every weekend we _____¹¹ our apartment. I also _____¹² at the supermarket.

Fernando _____¹³ soccer with his friends, and Claudio and I _____¹⁴ basketball.

What languages _____¹⁵ YOU speak? What do YOU _____¹⁶ every day?

G LISTENING

Listen and circle the word you hear.

1. (live)   lives
2. do   does
3. do   does
4. listen   listens
5. watch   watches
6. eat   eats
7. sing   sings
8. eat   eats
9. read   reads

H WHAT'S THE WORD?

do does	cook drive live paint sell

1. A. Where _____*does*_____ he live?

   B. He _____*lives*_____ in San Francisco.

2. A. What _____ they do?

   B. They _____ houses.

3. A. What _____ he do?

   B. He _____ a bus.

4. A. Where _____ you live?

   B. I _____ in Sydney.

5. A. What _____ you do?

   B. We _____ in a restaurant.

6. A. What _____ he _____?

   B. He _____ cars.

I WHAT'S THE DIFFERENCE?

1. I drive a bus. My friend Carla _____*drives*_____ a taxi.

2. We _____ in a bank. They work in an office.

3. Victor _____ the violin. His children play the piano.

4. I sell cars. My wife _____ computers.

5. I paint houses. My brother _____ pictures.

6. We live in Los Angeles. Our son _____ in London.

J LISTEN AND PRONOUNCE

Listen to each word and then say it.

1. chair	4. Chen	7. church	10. children	13. Sharp	16. Shirley	19. short
2. bench	5. kitchen	8. cheap	11. Richard	14. shirt	17. washing	20. English
3. Charlie	6. Chinese	9. watch	12. shoes	15. machine	18. station	21. French

K LOUD AND CLEAR 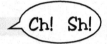 Ch! Sh!

Fill in the words. Then read the sentences aloud.

chair	Charlie	kitchen	Chinese

1. ____Charlie____ is sitting in a ____chair____ in his

_____ and eating _____ food.

Shirley	short	shoes

2. _____ isn't _____ in her new

_____.

watch	Richard	cheap	French

3. _____ is looking for a _____

_____ _____.

shirt	washing	washing machine

4. He's _____ his _____ in his

_____ _____.

bench	children	Chen	church

5. Mr. _____ and his _____ are sitting

on a _____ in front of the _____.

Sharp	station	English

6. Mr. _____ is in London at an _____

train _____.

1. Monday _____Tuesday_____ Wednesday

2. Friday _____ Sunday

3. Tuesday _____ Thursday   5. Thursday _____ Saturday

4. Saturday _____ Monday   6. Sunday _____ Tuesday

B WHAT ARE THEY SAYING?

Yes, { he / she / it } does. No, { he / she / it } doesn't.

what kind of
when

1. ___Does___ your husband cook breakfast every day?

Yes, _____he does_____.

2. _____ your daughter study English in school?

Yes, _____.

3. _____ your son drive a car?

No, _____.

4. _____ food does he cook?

He cooks Italian food.

5. _____ that dog live in this neighborhood?

No, it _____.

6. _____ your grandfather shop at the grocery store in his neighborhood?

Yes, _____.

7. _____ your sister work at the bank?

No, _____.

8. _____ does Robert visit his friends?

He visits his friends on Sunday.

C **WHAT ARE THEY SAYING?**

Yes, { I / we / you / they } do.   No, { I / we / you / they } don't.

1. __Do__ you sing in the shower?

Yes, __I do__.

2. _____ your children speak French?

No, _____.

3. _____ you and your husband live in this neighborhood?

Yes, _____.

4. _____ you and your wife play cards?

No, _____.

5. _____ you work on Saturday?

No, _____.

6. _____ your neighbors make a lot of noise?

Yes, _____.

D **LISTENING**

Listen and choose the correct response.

1. a. Chinese music.
   b. French food.
   c. Every day.

2. a. Yes, he does.
   b. No, we don't.
   c. Yes, they do.

3. a. No, he doesn't.
   b. Because he likes the food.
   c. On Wednesday.

4. a. On Sunday.
   b. Yes, she does.
   c. In her house.

5. a. I go every day.
   b. I don't go there.
   c. Yes, I do.

6. a. In New York.
   b. On Thursday.
   c. They don't go there.

7. a. Because it's open.
   b. They play.
   c. He rides his bicycle.

8. a. No, they don't.
   b. In the city.
   c. Yes, she does.

9. a. Because it's near their house.
   b. On Central Avenue.
   c. Yes, they do.

E YES AND NO

1. My husband cooks Italian food. He __doesn't__ __cook__ Thai food.

2. Linda drives a taxi. She _____ _____ a bus.

3. Our children play the piano. They _____ _____ the guitar.

4. I work on Saturday. I _____ _____ on Sunday.

5. Tom lives in an apartment. He _____ _____ in a house.

6. My wife and I exercise in the park. We _____ _____ in a health club.

7. Every Saturday Mrs. Roberts _____ to the library. She doesn't go to the mall.

8. I _____ in large supermarkets. I don't shop in small grocery stores.

9. My mother _____ stockings. She doesn't wear socks.

10. Omar _____ Arabic. He doesn't speak Spanish.

11. Harry sings in the shower. He _____ _____ in the jacuzzi.

F WHAT'S THE WORD?

do	does

1. Where ___do___ they live?

2. When _____ your daughter do her homework?

3. What kind of books _____ you read?

4. Why _____ he call you every day?

5. What languages _____ they speak?

6. Where _____ your husband work?

7. _____ you visit your friends every week?

8. _____ he go to Stanley's Restaurant?

9. When _____ you go to the supermarket?

10. _____ your children wash the dishes?

11. What kind of music _____ she listen to?

12. What _____ he sell?

13. Why _____ they cry at weddings?

G WRITE ABOUT YOURSELF

1. I like .... I don't like ....

2. I play .... I don't play ....

3. I speak .... I don't speak ....

4. I eat .... I don't eat ....

5. I cook .... I don't cook ....

1. Does Kathy take karate lessons?

   Yes, she does.

2. Do Jim and Tom play tennis on Sunday?

   No, they don't. They play volleyball.

3. Do you and Harry go dancing on Friday?

   _____

4. Does Miguel play in the orchestra?

   _____

5. Do you see a movie every weekend?

   _____

6. Do Mr. and Mrs. Kim go to a health club?

   _____

7. Does Richard jog in the park?

   _____

8. Do you and your wife watch TV every day?

   _____

I LISTENING

Listen and choose the correct response.

1. a. Yes, they do.
   b. Yes, I do. *(circled)*

2. a. Yes, he does.
   b. Yes, I do.

3. a. No, he doesn't.
   b. No, they don't.

4. a. No, she doesn't.
   b. No, I don't.

5. a. Yes, we do.
   b. Yes, he does.

6. a. Yes, we do.
   b. No, they don't.

7. a. No, I don't.
   b. Yes, he does.

8. a. Yes, they do.
   b. Yes, he does.

9. a. No, we don't.
   b. No, they don't.

J **GRAMMARRAP:** *They Do, They Don't*

Listen. Then clap and practice.

Does he	Yes he	No he

A. Does he eat French   bread?

B.   Yes, he   does.

A. Does she like Swiss   cheese?

B.   Yes, she   does.

A. Do they cook Greek   food?

B.   Yes, they   do.

A. Do they speak   Chinese?

B.   Yes, they   do.

All.   He eats French   bread.

      She likes Swiss   cheese.

      They cook Greek   food.

  And they speak   Chinese.

A. Does he read the   paper?

B.   No, he   doesn't.

A. Does she watch   TV?

B.   No, she   doesn't.

A. Do they go to   movies?

B.   No, they   don't.

A. Do they drink iced   tea?

B.   No, they   don't.

All.   He doesn't read the paper.

      She doesn't watch   TV.

      They don't go to   movies.

  And they don't drink   tea.

Activity Workbook   **73**

K A LETTER TO A PEN PAL

Read and practice.

                                                            Wednesday
Dear Peter,

   My family and I live in San Juan. We speak Spanish. My mother is a music teacher. She plays the violin and the piano. My father works in an office.

   My brother Ramon and I go to school every day. We study history, English, Spanish, science, and mathematics. My favorite school subject is science. I don't like history, but I like mathematics.

   Do you like sports? Every day at school I play soccer. On Saturday I swim. What sports do you play? What kind of music do you like? I like rock music and country music very much, but I don't like jazz. What kind of movies do you like? I like adventure movies and comedies. I think science fiction movies are terrible.

   Tell me about your family and your school.

                                                            Your friend,
                                                            Maria

L YOUR LETTER TO A PEN PAL

history
English
mathematics
science
music

baseball
football
hockey
golf
tennis
soccer

cartoons
dramas
comedies
westerns
adventure movies
science fiction
    movies

classical music
jazz
popular music
rock music
country music

Dear ....,

   My family and I live in .... We speak

.... At school, I study ....,

............................., and .... My favorite subject is

.... I don't like ....

   What sports do you play? I play .... and

.... I think .... is wonderful. I don't

like ....

   What kind of movies do you like? I like .... and

....

   My favorite kind of music is ...., and I like

.... I don't listen to ....

   Tell me about your school and your city.

                                                            Your friend,

                                                            ....

✓ CHECK-UP TEST: Chapters 9–10

A. Circle the correct answers.

Ex. We (live) / lives in Tokyo.

1. Tom **play** / **plays** in the park.

2. My wife and I **shop** / **shops** on Monday.

3. She **don't** / **doesn't** work on Saturday.

4. Where **do** / **does** your cousins live?

5. We **stays** / **stay** home every Sunday.

6. What activities **do** / **does** she do?

B. Fill in the blanks.

Ex. __What__ is your address?

1. _____ does he live?

2. _____ kind of food do you like?

3. _____ Patty baby-sit for her neighbors?

4. _____ do you eat at that restaurant?
   Because we like the food.

5. _____ does Julie go to a health club?
   On Monday.

6. _____ does your family do on Sunday?

C. Fill in the blanks.

Mrs. Davis _____¹ in Dallas. She's a very active person. She _____² exercises every day. On Monday she _____³ her apartment, on Wednesday she _____⁴ tennis, on Friday she _____⁵ a karate lesson, on Saturday she _____⁶ her bicycle in the park, and on Sunday she _____⁷ to a museum and _____⁸ lunch in a restaurant.

D. Listen and choose the correct response.

Ex. a. We go to school.
   (b.) They work in an office.
   c. They're shy.

1. a. Yes, we do.
   b. We like dramas.
   c. On Thursday.

2. a. In a restaurant.
   b. Because we like it.
   c. Every day.

3. a. Yes, they do.
   b. Yes, he does.
   c. In Puerto Rico.

4. a. Short stories.
   b. News programs.
   c. I like golf.

5. a. Yes, they do.
   b. Because it's convenient.
   c. On Center Street.

Read the article on student book page 97 and answer the questions.

1. There are _____ languages in the world.
   a. five hundred
   b. millions of
   c. twenty thousand
   d. more than twenty thousand

2. _____ is a very rare language.
   a. Chinese
   b. Spanish
   c. Bahinemo
   d. Arabic

3. The word *ketchup* is from _____.
   a. Chinese
   b. French
   c. Spanish
   d. Arabic

4. The word *cyberspace* comes from _____.
   a. French
   b. Spanish
   c. Arabic
   d. technology

5. The word _____ is from Arabic.
   a. *rodeo*
   b. *sofa*
   c. *potato*
   d. *cafe*

6. According to this article, Portuguese is a _____ language.
   a. difficult
   b. common
   c. rare
   d. new

7. Bahinemo is a language from _____.
   a. China
   b. the United States
   c. Japan
   d. Papua, New Guinea

8. *Borrow* in paragraph 2 means _____.
   a. speak
   b. study
   c. take
   d. give

9. *Recent* in paragraph 2 means _____.
   a. new
   b. difficult
   c. interesting
   d. common

10. _____ is a recent word.
    a. *Ketchup*
    b. *Website*
    c. *Potato*
    d. *Rodeo*

STUDENT BOOK
PAGES **97–98**

B **BUILD YOUR VOCABULARY!**

Choose the correct word.

1. I comb my (hair   teeth).

2. She (goes   gets) up, and then she (goes   gets) dressed.

3. I sit and relax when I take a (shower   bath).

4. He (eats   brushes his teeth) after breakfast, lunch, and dinner.

5. She (takes   cleans) a shower every morning.

6. I don't get (dressed   up) on Sunday morning. I eat breakfast in my pajamas.

7. Rosa goes to (work   bed) at 12:00 every night and gets up at 7:00.

8. Martin cooks in a restaurant on weekends. He goes to (work   school) every Saturday and Sunday.

9. Tina doesn't eat breakfast because she (gets up   goes to bed) late.

C FACT FILE

Look at the Fact File on student book page 97 and answer the questions.

1. Three hundred twenty-two million people speak _____.
   a. Russian
   b. Arabic
   c. Spanish
   d. English

2. One hundred eighty-two million people speak _____.
   a. Japanese
   b. Bengali
   c. Hindi
   d. Portuguese

3. There are _____ Arabic speakers.
   a. three hundred thirty-two million
   b. two hundred sixty-eight million
   c. one hundred seventy million
   d. eight hundred eighty-five million

4. More than three hundred million people speak _____.
   a. Russian
   b. Bengali
   c. Spanish
   d. Arabic

5. There are _____ Japanese speakers.
   a. one hundred twenty-five million
   b. one hundred eighty-nine million
   c. ninety-eight million
   d. one hundred eighty-nine million

6. There are the same number of Portuguese and _____ speakers.
   a. German
   b. Bengali
   c. Hindi
   d. Russian

7. More than eight hundred million people speak _____.
   a. English
   b. Chinese
   c. Hindi and Portuguese
   d. Arabic and Bengali

8. Spanish and _____ are common languages in South America.
   a. Portuguese
   b. Japanese
   c. Bengali
   d. Arabic

D "CAN-DO" REVIEW

Match the "can do" statement and the correct sentence.

____ 1. I can ask a person's name.

____ 2. I can tell where I live.

____ 3. I can tell what language I speak.

____ 4. I can tell about my nationality.

____ 5. I can tell about my work.

____ 6. I can ask about a person's work.

____ 7. I can talk about likes.

____ 8. I can talk about dislikes.

____ 9. I can describe people.

____ 10. I can ask questions to make small talk.

a. I speak Spanish.

b. I drive a bus.

c. My sister is an outgoing person.

d. I like Greek food.

e. I live in Seoul.

f. I don't like American food.

g. I'm Mexican.

h. What kind of music do you like?

i. What do you do?

j. What's your name?

A WHAT ARE THEY SAYING?

me	us
him	you
her	them
it	

1. Do you like me?

Of course I like __you__.

2. Do you like your neighbors?

Of course I like _____.

3. Do you like Helen?

Of course I like _____.

4. Do you like George?

Of course I like _____.

5. Do you like videos?

Of course I like _____.

6. Do you like English?

Of course I like _____.

7. Do your friends like you?

Of course they like _____.

8. Do you like your new apartment?

Of course I like _____.

9. Does your dog like you?

Of course he likes _____.

B WHAT'S THE WORD?

it	her	him	them

1. She washes ___it___ every morning.

2. I think about _____ all the time.

3. We visit _____ every weekend.

4. I talk to _____ every night.

5. He uses _____ every day.

6. We feed _____ every afternoon.

C LISTENING

Listen and put a check (✓) under the correct picture.

1. _____ ✔

2. _____ _____

3. _____ _____

4. _____ _____

5. _____ _____

6. _____ _____

D WRITE ABOUT YOURSELF

1. I .... every day.

2. I .... every week.

3. I .... every month.

4. I .... every year.

5. I .... every weekend.

6. I .... every Sunday.

7. I .... every morning.

8. I .... all the time.

E WRITE IT AND SAY IT

Write the correct form of the word in parentheses and then say the sentence.

1. Carol sometimes (eat) ___eats___ Thai food.

2. My neighbor's dog always (bark) _____ in the afternoon.

3. My son never (clean) _____ his bedroom.

4. Ray always (wash) _____ his car on the weekend.

5. My brother sometimes (jog) _____ at night.

6. Amy usually (read) _____ poetry.

7. My mother rarely (shop) _____ at the grocery store around the corner.

8. Dan sometimes (watch) _____ videos on Saturday.

9. Omar usually (speak) _____ English at work.

10. Patty usually (play) _____ tennis in the park on Saturday.

F MATCHING

_c_	1. Walter always washes his car on Sunday.	a.	She usually watches dramas.
____	2. Jonathan never cooks dinner.	b.	He rarely jogs at night.
____	3. Carla rarely watches comedies.	c.	He never washes it during the week.
____	4. My grandmother rarely speaks English.	d.	She usually studies in the library.
____	5. Richard usually jogs in the morning.	e.	He always eats in a restaurant.
____	6. Larry never writes letters.	f.	He always writes e-mail messages.
____	7. Nancy rarely studies at home.	g.	She usually speaks Spanish.
____	8. Jane always fixes her computer.	h.	She never calls a repairperson.

G LISTENING

Listen and choose the correct answer.

1. a. He usually washes it.
   b. He never washes it.

2. a. My husband sometimes cooks.
   b. My husband never cooks.

3. a. My neighbors are quiet.
   b. My neighbors are noisy.

4. a. They usually speak Spanish.
   b. They usually speak English.

5. a. Jane is shy.
   b. Jane is outgoing.

6. a. I usually study at home.
   b. I usually study in the library.

WRITE ABOUT YOURSELF

always	usually	sometimes	rarely	never

1. I .... wear glasses.
2. I .... eat Italian food.
3. I .... listen to country music.
4. I .... go to English class.
5. I .... watch videos.
6. I .... read poetry.
7. I .... fix my car.
8. I .... visit my grandparents.

9. I .... watch game shows on TV.
10. I .... use a cell phone.
11. I .... clean my apartment.
12. I always ....
13. I usually ....
14. I sometimes ....
15. I rarely ....
16. I never ....

I **GRAMMARRAP:** *I Always Get to Work on Time*

Listen. Then clap and practice.

A.   I always get to   work on time.

        I'm usually here by   eight.

        I sometimes get here   early.

        I never get here   late.

        No, I never get here   late.

B.   He always gets to   work on time.

        He's usually here by   eight.

        He sometimes gets here early.

        He rarely gets here   late.

A.   No! I NEVER get here   late.

B.   Right! He never gets here   late.

WHAT'S THE WORD?

have	has

1. Do you ___have___ a bicycle?

2. My daughter _____ curly hair.

3. My parents _____ an old car.

4. Does your son _____ blond hair?

5. Our building _____ a satellite dish.

6. Do you _____ large sunglasses?

7. My sister _____ green eyes.

8. We _____ two dogs and a cat.

K **WHAT ARE THEY SAYING?**

have	has	do	does	don't	doesn't

1. ___Does___ your son ___have___ a bicycle?

   No. He ___doesn't___ ___have___ a bicycle. He __has__ a motorcycle.

2. Do you have short stories?

   No. We _____ _____ short stories, but we _____ novels.

3. Do your children _____ a good teacher?

   Yes. They _____ a wonderful teacher.

4. What kind of computer _____ you _____?

   I _____ a Dell.

5. _____ they _____ jeans?

   No. They _____ _____ jeans, but they _____ jackets.

6. _____ this store _____ an elevator?

   No. It _____ _____ an elevator, but it _____ an escalator.

L WHAT'S THE WORD?

1. Tina doesn't have short hair. She has (long) / curly hair.

2. I don't have straight hair. I have thin / curly hair.

3. My brother isn't tall. He's heavy / short .

4. Albert isn't married. He's curly / single .

5. Your baby boy has beautiful blond eyes / hair .

6. His eyes aren't blue. They're brown / straight .

7. We don't live in the city. We live in the house / suburbs .

M TWO BROTHERS

My brother and I are very different. I'm tall, and he's ___short___ 1. I _____ 2 brown

eyes, and he _____ 3 blue eyes. We both _____ 4 brown hair, but I have long, straight

hair, and he has _____ 5, _____ 6 hair. I'm short and heavy. And he's _____ 7

and _____ 8. I'm a chef, and _____ 9 a doctor. I live in New York. He _____ 10 in

San Diego. I have a small apartment in the city. He _____ 11 a large house _____ 12 the

suburbs. I play tennis. He _____ 13 golf. I play the guitar. He doesn't _____ 14 a musical

instrument. On the weekend, I usually _____ 15 to parties. He doesn't _____ 16 to parties.

He _____ 17 TV and _____ 18 the newspaper.

N · LISTENING 🔊

Listen and choose the correct response.

1. a. No. I have short hair.
   b. No. I have straight hair. *(circled)*

2. a. No. I'm single.
   b. No. I'm tall and thin.

3. a. No. He has black eyes.
   b. No. He has brown eyes.

4. a. No. This is my mother.
   b. No. I have a sister.

5. a. Yes. I go to parties.
   b. Yes. I stay home.

6. a. Yes. He's thin.
   b. No. He's thin.

7. a. No. I live in an apartment.
   b. No. I live in the suburbs.

8. a. No. I have long hair.
   b. No. I have curly hair.

O · WHAT'S THE WORD?

Circle the correct word.

1. He watches TV [at / with / (in)] the evening.

2. The health club is [in / on / between] Main Street.

3. I'm playing a game [on / to / in] my computer.

4. Ann is sleeping [on / in / across] the yard.

5. He always talks [about / to / with] the weather.

6. I'm looking [from / for / to] a striped shirt.

7. Do you live [in / on / at] the suburbs?

8. Do your children go [to / at / in] school every day?

9. Tim is swimming [with / on / at] the beach.

10. My son is wearing a pair [from / for / of] new jeans.

11. Do you go [in / to / at] work [at / in / on] Saturday?

12. I listen [to / at / on] the radio in the morning.

82   Activity Workbook

A WHAT'S THE WORD?

STUDENT BOOK
PAGES 107–114

| angry | embarrassed | hot | nervous | scared | thirsty |
| cold | happy | hungry | sad | sick | tired |

1. Howard is crying. He's _____sad_____.

2. Helen is yawning. She's _____.

3. Sam is perspiring. He's _____.

4. Frank is shouting. He's _____.

5. Mrs. Allen is going to the hospital.

   She's _____.

6. Peter is looking at his paper and smiling.

   He's _____.

7. Ben's cat is eating. It's _____.

8. Irene is shivering. She's _____.

9. Louise is biting her nails.

   She's _____.

10. Jason is covering his eyes.

   He's _____.

11. Pam is drinking milk.

   She's _____.

12. Bobby is blushing.

   He's _____.

Activity Workbook   83

1. A. Why are they yawning?

   B. <u>They're yawning because they're</u> tired.

   They always <u>yawn when they're tired</u>.

3. A. Why is he shivering?

   B. _____ cold.

   He always _____.

5. A. Why is she smiling?

   B. _____ happy.

   She always _____.

7. A. Why are you shouting?

   B. _____ angry.

   We always _____.

2. A. Why is she crying?

   B. _____ sad.

   She always _____.

4. A. Why are you perspiring?

   B. _____ hot.

   I always _____.

6. A. Why are they eating?

   B. _____ hungry.

   They always _____.

8. A. Why is he covering his eyes?

   B. _____ scared.

   He always _____.

C GRAMMARRAP: *I Smile When I'm Happy*

Listen. Then clap and practice.

A.　　I smile when I'm　　happy.

I frown when I'm　　sad.

I blush when I'm　embarrassed.

And I shout when I'm　　mad.

B.　Are you smiling?

A.　Yes. I'm happy.

B.　Are you frowning?

A.　Yes. I'm sad.

B.　Are you blushing?

A.　I'm embarrassed.

B.　Are you shouting?

A.　Yes. I'm mad.

D GRAMMARRAP: *Why Are You Doing That?*

Listen. Then clap and practice.

A.　　What's Fran　　doing?

B.　She's working　　late.

A.　　Working　　late?

Why's she doing　that?

B.　It's Monday.

She always works　late on　　Monday.

A.　What are you　　doing?

B.　We're playing　　cards.

A.　Playing　　cards?

Why are you doing　that?

B.　It's Tuesday.

We always play　cards on　　Tuesday.

Activity Workbook　　**85**

A. What's Bob doing?

B. He's cooking spaghetti.

A. Cooking spaghetti?
   Why's he doing that?

B. It's Wednesday.
   He always cooks spaghetti on Wednesday.

A. What's Maria doing?

B. She's dancing.

A. Dancing?
   Why's she doing that?

B. It's Thursday.
   She always dances on Thursday.

A. What's Gary doing?

B. He's bathing his cat.

A. Bathing his cat?
   Why's he doing that?

B. It's Friday.
   He always bathes his cat on Friday.

A. What are you doing?

B. I'm _____ing.

A. _____?
   Why are you doing that?

B. It's Saturday.
   I always _____ on Saturday.

1. A. My sister is cooking dinner today.

   B. That's strange! She never ___cooks___ dinner.

2. A. Our children are studying with a flashlight.
   B. That's strange! They never _____ with a flashlight.

3. A. Victor is walking to work today.

   B. That's strange! He never _____ to work.

4. A. Ann is brushing her teeth in the kitchen.

   B. That's strange! She never _____ her teeth in the kitchen.

5. A. The dog is eating in the dining room today.
   B. That's strange! It never _____ in the dining room.

6. A. Nancy and Bob are dancing in the office.
   B. That's strange! They never _____ in the office.

7. A. Ruth _____ the carpet today.
   B. That's strange! She never sweeps the carpet.

8. A. My parents _____ poetry today.
   B. That's strange! They never read poetry.

9. A. _____ a typewriter today.

   B. That's strange! You never use a typewriter.

10. A. My cousins _____ in the yard.
    B. That's strange! They never sleep in the yard.

F WHAT'S THE QUESTION?

Choose the correct question word. Then write the question.

What	When	Where	Why	What kind of	How many

1. I'm blushing <u>because I'm embarrassed</u>. _____ *Why are you blushing?* _____

2. They play tennis <u>in the park</u>. _____

3. She reads her e-mail <u>at night</u>. _____

4. I like <u>Brazilian</u> food. _____

5. We have <u>ten</u> cats. _____

6. He's using his <u>cell phone</u>. _____

What	How often	Where	Why	What kind of	How many

7. He watches <u>game</u> shows. _____

8. We call our grandchildren <u>every week</u>. _____

9. They <u>play golf</u> every weekend. _____

10. I'm smiling <u>because I'm happy</u>. _____

11. She's eating <u>in the cafeteria</u> today. _____

12. I'm wearing <u>two</u> sweaters. _____

G WHICH ONE DOESN'T BELONG?

#				
1.	her	me	them	(we)
2.	noisy	usually	sometimes	rarely
3.	does	doesn't	has	don't
4.	angry	yoga	nervous	happy
5.	Wednesday	Why	What	When
6.	smiling	shivering	crying	outgoing
7.	clean	sweep	shy	wash
8.	year	evening	night	afternoon

LISTENING

As you listen to each story, read the sentences and check *yes* or *no*.

Jennifer and Jason

1. yes ☐ no ☑   Jennifer and Jason are visiting their father.
2. yes ☐ no ☐   Jennifer and Jason are happy.
3. yes ☐ no ☐   Their grandfather isn't taking them to the park.

Our Boss

4. yes ☐ no ☐   Our boss usually smiles at the office.
5. yes ☐ no ☐   He's happy today.
6. yes ☐ no ☐   Everyone is thinking about the weekend.

On Vacation

7. yes ☐ no ☐   I like vacations.
8. yes ☐ no ☐   When the weather is nice, I watch videos.
9. yes ☐ no ☐   I'm swimming at the beach today because it's cold.

Timmy and His Brother

10. yes ☐ no ☐   Timmy is covering his eyes because he's sad.
11. yes ☐ no ☐   Timmy doesn't like science fiction movies.
12. yes ☐ no ☐   Timmy's brother is scared.

I **LOUD AND CLEAR** S! Z!

| sorry hospital sick sister Sally | scientist speaking What's experiments |

1. ____Sally____ is ____sorry____ her

____sister____ is ____sick____ in

the ___hospital___.

2. _____ the _____ doing?

He's _____ about his new

_____.

always	cousin	Athens	busy	is

3. My _____ in _____

_____ _____ very

_____.

doesn't	Sally's	clothes	husband	closet

4. _____ _____ _____

have any clean _____ in his

_____.

Steven	it's	sweeping	is	because

5. _____ _____ _____

the floor _____ _____ dirty.

Sunday	Mrs.	newspaper	Garcia	reads

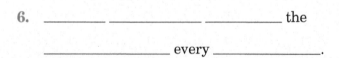

6. _____ _____ _____ the

_____ every _____.

zoo	students	sometimes	bus	school

7. The _____ in our

_____ _____ go

to the _____ on the _____.

plays	soccer	friends	Tuesday	son

8. My _____ Sam _____

_____ with his _____

every _____.

A. Fill in the blanks.

| me | him | her | it | us | you | them |

Ex. Do you like this book?
Of course I like ___it___.

1. Do you look like your father?
Yes. I look like _____.

2. When my cats are hungry, I always feed
_____.

3. Sally rarely plays with her sister, but she's
playing with _____ today.

4. I say "hello" to my boss every day, and he
says "hello" to _____.

5. We're going to the park. Do you want to go
with _____?

B. Fill in the blanks.

Ex. Betty never talks to her landlord, but
she's ___talking___ to him today.

1. We never feed the birds, but we're
_____ them today.

2. Harriet never _____ to parties, but
she's going to a party today.

3. My children never bake, but they're
_____ today.

4. Tim never _____ his TV, but he's
fixing it today.

5. Amy rarely _____ her kitchen
windows, but she's washing them today.

C. Fill in the blanks.

| do | does | is | are |

Ex. a. What ___do___ you usually do on the
weekend?

b. What ___is___ Tina doing today?

1. Why _____ the baby crying?

2. When _____ David and Pam go to the
supermarket?

3. _____ Bob usually dance?

4. Do they work here? Yes, they _____.

5. _____ your parents cooking lunch?

D. Write the question.

Ex. I'm shivering because I'm cold. (Why?)
___Why are you shivering?___

1. They work in a laboratory every day.
(Where?)
_____

2. We get together on Saturday. (When?)
_____

3. He's crying because he's sad. (Why?)
_____

4. She has three children. (How many?)
_____

5. I'm drinking milk. (What?)
_____

E. Listen and choose the correct response.

Ex. a. They're playing soccer.
b. They play tennis.

1. a. They're delivering mail.
b. They deliver mail.

2. a. We're going to the zoo.
b. We go to the park.

3. a. I'm covering my eyes.
b. I cover my eyes.

4. a. No, I don't.
b. No, I'm not.

5. a. I'm studying in the library.
b. I study in the library.

Read the article on student book page 115 and answer the questions.

SIDE
by SIDE
Gazette

STUDENT BOOK
PAGES 115–116

1. Rush hour is the time when _____.
   a. people are busy at work
   b. people are busy at home
   c. people go to work
   d. the roads are empty

2. Some _____ have carpool lanes.
   a. bus systems
   b. highways
   c. subway systems
   d. license plates

3. Carpool lanes are for _____.
   a. cars with two or more people
   b. cars with special license plates
   c. all cars during rush hour
   d. cars on two or three days of the week

4. *Cities are expanding their bus and subway systems* means _____.
   a. cities are painting them
   b. cities are cleaning them
   c. cities are fixing them
   d. there are more and more buses and subways in these cities

5. Many cities are trying to reduce _____.
   a. the traffic on their roads
   b. their highways

   c. their carpool lanes
   d. their bus and subway systems

6. Traffic is a big problem in cities around the world because many people _____.
   a. take buses to work
   b. drive to work
   c. take trains to work
   d. take subways to work

7. In Athens people with license plate numbers ending in 4 _____.
   a. drive their cars four days a week
   b. drive their cars every day of the week
   c. drive their cars in special lanes
   d. don't drive their cars every day of the week

8. *Traffic is a global problem* means _____.
   a. traffic is a problem in Athens
   b. traffic is a difficult problem
   c. traffic is a problem around the world
   d. traffic is a problem today

B **BUILD YOUR VOCABULARY!**

Choose the correct word.

1. My office is around the corner from my house so I (walk   take the bus) to work.

2. I ride a (motorcycle   bicycle) to work because it's a good way to exercise.

3. I live in the suburbs and take the (train   subway) to work. I sit at a window and I look at the people and houses outside.

4. I (ride a motor scooter   drive) to work. It's a good way to get there except when it rains.

5. I take the (subway   bus) to work. When there's a lot of traffic it takes thirty minutes.

6. I (ride a motorcycle   drive) to work. It's noisy, but it's fun in good weather.

7. Sometimes when I'm very late for work I (ride a bicycle   take a taxi).

8. I (drive   walk) to work on a very busy highway.

9. I (ride a motor scooter   take the subway) to work. Sometimes there are a lot of people, and there isn't a place to sit.

Look at the Fact File on student book page 116 and answer the questions.

1. More than seven hundred million people ride the subway in São Paulo in a _____.
   a. month
   b. year
   c. week
   d. day

2. Seven hundred seventy-nine million people ride the subway in _____ in a year.
   a. Hong Kong
   b. Tokyo
   c. São Paulo
   d. London

3. _____ people ride the subway in Moscow in a year.
   a. 3,160
   b. 31,600
   c. 3,160,000
   d. 3,160,000,000

4. The largest subway systems in the world have _____ riders.
   a. hundreds of
   b. thousands of
   c. a million
   d. millions of

5. The subway system in Seoul has 1,390,000,000 riders, but the subway system in _____ has even more riders.
   a. London
   b. Mexico City
   c. Hong Kong
   d. Paris

6. The subway system in _____ has 1,000,000,000 riders.
   a. Tokyo
   b. New York
   c. Osaka
   d. Paris

7. _____ people ride the subway in Paris in a year.
   a. 1,120,000,000
   b. 1,420,000,000
   c. 2,740,000,000
   d. 1,130,000,000

8. Two of the world's largest subway systems are in _____.
   a. Russia
   b. England
   c. Japan
   d. Mexico

D "CAN-DO" REVIEW

Match the "can do" statement and the correct sentence.

_____ 1. I can talk about common activities.

_____ 2. I can describe people.

_____ 3. I can give my occupation.

_____ 4. I can give my marital status.

_____ 5. I can ask for information.

_____ 6. I can react to information.

_____ 7. I can describe my emotions.

_____ 8. I can ask about a person's activity.

_____ 9. I can describe a repair problem.

_____ 10. I can describe how I react to things.

a. Tell me about your children.

b. I'm a scientist.

c. Oh, really? That's interesting.

d. What are you doing?

e. I'm happy.

f. My computer is broken.

g. I usually watch the news after dinner.

h. I'm single.

i. When I'm embarrassed, I blush.

j. My sister has short, curly hair.

cook	drive	play	skate	speak
dance	paint	sing	ski	use

1. Billy <u>can't</u> <u>ski</u>.

   He <u>can</u> <u>skate</u>.

2. Sally _____ _____.

   She _____ _____.

3. Edward _____ _____ pictures.

   He _____ _____ houses.

4. Carla _____ _____ Arabic.

   She _____ _____ Italian.

5. We _____ _____ Greek food.

   We _____ _____ Japanese food.

6. I _____ _____ a cash register.

   I _____ _____ a calculator.

7. They _____ _____ tennis.

   They _____ _____ baseball.

8. Harold _____ _____ a taxi.

   He _____ _____ a bus.

B WHAT CAN YOU DO?

Check the things you can do. Then ask other students.

Can you . . .?	You		Student 1		Student 2	
1. cook	❏ yes	❏ no	❏ yes	❏ no	❏ yes	❏ no
2. swim	❏ yes	❏ no	❏ yes	❏ no	❏ yes	❏ no
3. ski	❏ yes	❏ no	❏ yes	❏ no	❏ yes	❏ no
4. skate	❏ yes	❏ no	❏ yes	❏ no	❏ yes	❏ no
5. paint	❏ yes	❏ no	❏ yes	❏ no	❏ yes	❏ no
6. drive	❏ yes	❏ no	❏ yes	❏ no	❏ yes	❏ no
7. play tennis	❏ yes	❏ no	❏ yes	❏ no	❏ yes	❏ no
8. speak Chinese	❏ yes	❏ no	❏ yes	❏ no	❏ yes	❏ no
9. use a cash register	❏ yes	❏ no	❏ yes	❏ no	❏ yes	❏ no

C WHAT'S THE QUESTION?

1. _____Can he cook_____?   2. _____?   3. _____?

Yes, he can.   No, she can't.   Yes, they can.

4. _____?   5. _____?   6. _____?

Yes, I can.   No, he can't.   No, we can't.

D LISTENING

Listen and circle the word you hear.

1. (can)   can't   4. can   can't   7. can   can't   10. can   can't

2. can   can't   5. can   can't   8. can   can't   11. can   can't

3. can   can't   6. can   can't   9. can   can't   12. can   can't

PUZZLE

| actor | actress | baker | chef | dancer | mechanic | secretary | singer | teacher | truck driver |

Across

4. She fixes cars every day.
6. He teaches in a school.
7. She acts in the movies.
9. He dances every day.
10. He acts on TV.

Down

1. She drives a truck.
2. He types every day.
3. He cooks in a restaurant.
5. He bakes pies and cakes.
8. She sings on TV.

F **CAN OR _CAN'T_?**

1. My brother is a chef in a bakery. He ____can____ bake pies and cakes.

2. They ____can't____ sing. They aren't very good singers.

3. _____ Jane drive a truck? Of course she _____.
   She's a truck driver.

4. The chef in that restaurant _____ cook!
   The food is terrible!

5. Of course I _____ fix cars. I'm a mechanic.

6. That actor is terrible! He _____ act!

7. _____ they dance? Of course they _____.
   They're dancers on TV.

8. I'm a very good cashier. I _____ use a cash register.

9. My new secretary isn't very good. He _____ type, and he _____ speak on the telephone.

10. They're very athletic. They _____ skate, they _____ ski, and they _____ play soccer.

11. My friend George can only speak English. He _____ speak Spanish, and he _____ speak French.

GRAMMARRAP: *Of Course They Can!*

Listen. Then clap and practice.

> She can speak.
> He can speak.
> We can speak.
> They can speak.

A. Can Anne speak French?

B. Of course she can.

   She can speak French very well.

A. Can the Browns play tennis?

B. Of course they can.

   They can play tennis very well.

A. Can Peter bake pies?

B. Of course he can.

   He can bake pies very well.

A. Can we speak English?

B. Of course we can.

   We can speak English very well.

WHAT ARE THEY SAYING?

have to	do	don't
has to	does	doesn't

1. Can you play baseball with me?

   I'm sorry. I can't. I <u>have</u> <u>to</u> do my homework.

2. Why is Susie upset today?

   She _____ _____ go to the dentist this afternoon.

3. Can your husband fix the sink?

   No, he can't. He _____ _____ call a plumber.

4. Do I really _____ _____ get a haircut?

   Yes, you do. You _____ _____ get a haircut today.

5. _____ Grandma _____ _____ go to the doctor often?

   Yes, she _____. She _____ _____ go to the doctor every month.

6. _____ you _____ _____ work today?

   No, I _____. I'm on vacation.

7. Do you want to go skiing this weekend?

   This weekend? Sorry. We can't.

   We _____ _____ clean our apartment.

8. Are you bored?

   No. I'm tired. I _____ _____ go to bed.

I A BUSY FAMILY

Mr. and Mrs. Lane, their son Danny, and their daughter Julie are very busy this week.

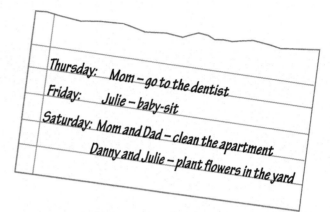

Monday: Dad – speak to the superintendent
            Mom – meet with Danny's teacher
Tuesday: Danny and Julie – go to the doctor
Wednesday: Dad – fix the car

Thursday: Mom – go to the dentist
Friday: Julie – baby-sit
Saturday: Mom and Dad – clean the apartment
          Danny and Julie – plant flowers in the yard

1. What does Mr. Lane have to do on Monday? _____He has to speak to the superintendent._____

2. What does Mrs. Lane have to do on Monday? _____

3. What do Danny and Julie have to do on Tuesday? _____

4. What does Mr. Lane have to do on Wednesday? _____

5. What does Mrs. Lane have to do on Thursday? _____

6. What does Julie have to do on Friday? _____

7. What do Mr. and Mrs. Lane have to do on Saturday? _____

8. What do Danny and Julie have to do on Saturday? _____

J WRITE ABOUT YOURSELF

What do YOU have to do this week?

....

....

....

....

K LISTENING

Listen and circle the words you hear.

1. has to   (have to)   4. has to   have to   7. can   can't

2. has to   have to   5. can   can't   8. has to   have to

3. can   can't   6. has to   have to   9. can   can't

Activity Workbook   **97**

L THEY'RE BUSY

can't	baby-sit	go swimming	have dinner
have to	clean the house	go to a movie	study
has to	go bowling	go to a soccer game	wash my clothes
	go dancing	go to the dentist	work

1. I _____can't go swimming_____ today.

   I _____have to go the dentist_____.

2. Patty _____ on Saturday.

   She _____.

3. Bob and Julie _____ today.

   They _____.

4. Tom _____ today.

   He _____.

5. We _____ on Saturday.

   We _____.

6. I _____ with you today.

   I _____.

M LISTENING

Listen and choose the correct answer.

1. a. She has to go to the dentist.
   b. She can go to the movies.

2. a. He has to wash his car.
   b. He can't go to the party.

3. a. She can have lunch with her friend.
   b. She can have dinner with her friend.

4. a. They have to paint their kitchen.
   b. They can go skiing.

5. a. He has to cook lunch.
   b. He has to go shopping today.

6. a. She has to baby-sit on Friday.
   b. She can't see a play on Saturday.

N GRAMMARRAP: *Where Is Everybody?*

Listen. Then clap and practice.

A. Where's   Joe?

B. He has to   go.

A. Where's   Ray?

B. He can't   stay.

A. Where's   Kate?

B. She can't   wait.

A. Where's   Steve?

B. He has to   leave.

A. Where's   Murray?

B. He has to   hurry.

A. What about   you?

B. I have to go, too.

All.   Oh,   no!

Joe has to   go.

Ray can't   stay.

Kate can't   wait.

Steve has to   leave.

Murray has to hurry.

What can I   do?

I have to go, too.

O GRAMMARRAP: *Can't Talk Now*

Listen. Then clap and practice.

A. I can't talk   now.

    I have to go to   work.

B. I can't stop   now.

    I have to catch a train.

C. I can't leave   now.

    I have to make a   call.

D. I can't stop   now.

    I have to catch a   plane.

All.   She can't stop   now.

       She has to catch a   train.

       She can't stop   now.

       She has to catch a   plane.

A WHAT ARE THEY GOING TO DO?

1. What's Larry going to do tomorrow?

   _____He's going to cook._____

2. What's Jane going to do tomorrow?

   _____

3. What are you going to do tomorrow?

   _____

4. What are they going to do tomorrow?

   _____

5. What are you and your friends going to do tomorrow?

   _____

6. What's William going to do tomorrow?

   _____

B WHAT ARE THEY SAYING?

1. ___What are___ you

   ___going to do___ tomorrow?

   ___I'm going to___ clean my apartment.

3. _____ your mother

   _____ tomorrow?

   _____ plant flowers.

2. _____ your husband

   _____ tomorrow?

   _____ fix the kitchen sink.

4. _____ your cousins

   _____ tomorrow?

   _____ visit us.

100 Activity Workbook

C WHAT ARE THEY GOING TO DO?

are	is	going	go	to

1. We're ___going___ ___to___ ___go___ dancing tonight.

2. They're ___going___ swimming this afternoon.

3. I'm _____ _____ _____ shopping tomorrow.

4. Brian _____ _____ _____ the library this morning.

5. Rita _____ _____ _____ _____ _____ a party tomorrow night.

6. My friends and I _____ _____ to a baseball game tomorrow afternoon.

7. Mr. and Mrs. Lopez _____ _____ _____ _____ _____ a concert this evening.

8. I'm _____ _____ the supermarket tomorrow morning, and my husband

   _____ _____ _____ _____ _____ the bank.

D GRAMMARRAP: *What Are You Going to Do?*

Listen. Then clap and practice.

going to = gonna

All.　What are you going to　do tomorrow　morning?

　　　How about　　　tomorrow　　　afternoon?

　　　What are you going to　do tomorrow　evening?

　　　What are you going to　do this　　June?

A.　I'm going to vacuum all my　rugs tomorrow　morning.

B.　I'm going to walk my dog　tomorrow　afternoon.

C.　I'm going to visit all my　friends tomorrow　evening.

D.　I'm going to dance at my　wedding this　June.

E WHICH WORD DOESN'T BELONG?

1. January   May   (Monday)   April

2. Tuesday   Saturday   Sunday   September

3. autumn   at once   winter   summer

4. Friday   February   March   October

5. him   them   he   her

6. right now   next week   at once   immediately

F WHAT'S NEXT?

1. June   July   _August_   4. summer   fall   _____

2. Monday   Tuesday   _____   5. Friday   Saturday   _____

3. February March   _____   6. October   November   _____

G MATCH THE SENTENCES

Are you going to . . .

_c_ 1. call your friends on Thursday?   a. No. I'm going to visit them in October.

____ 2. fix our doorbell this week?   b. No. I'm going to visit her next winter.

____ 3. visit your aunt next summer?   c. No. I'm going to call them on Friday.

____ 4. visit your cousins in April?   d. No. I'm going to fix them next month.

____ 5. fix our windows this month?   e. No. I'm going to call him this July.

____ 6. call your uncle this June?   f. No. I'm going to fix it next week.

H LISTENING

Listen and circle the words you hear.

1. (this)   next   5. Tuesday   Thursday   9. autumn   August
2. right now   right away   6. November   December   10. watch   wash
3. Monday   Sunday   7. spring   winter   11. next   this
4. wash   cut   8. at once   next month   12. number   plumber

I WHAT'S THE QUESTION?

1. We're going to <u>do our exercises</u> right now.   What _____ *are you going to do right now?*

2. She's going to baby-sit <u>this Friday</u>.   When _____

3. We're going to <u>Paris</u> next April.   Where _____

4. I'm going to clean it <u>because it's dirty</u>.   Why _____

5. They're going to <u>go to the beach</u> today.   What _____

6. I'm going to fix the doorbell <u>next week</u>.   When _____

7. She's going to plant flowers <u>in her yard</u>.   Where _____

8. He's going to read his e-mail <u>right now</u>.   When _____

9. I'm going to bed now <u>because I'm tired</u>.   Why _____

J LISTENING 🔊

Listen to the following weather forecasts and circle the correct answers.

Today's Weather Forecast

| **This afternoon:** | hot | (cool) | sunny | (cloudy) |
| **This evening:** | foggy | clear | rain | warm |

This Weekend's Weather Forecast

Tonight:	cool	cold	clear	warm
Saturday:	cloudy	sunny	foggy	hot
Sunday:	foggy	cool	snow	rain

Monday's Weather Forecast

Monday morning:	cold	cool	cloudy	nice
Monday afternoon:	cool	cold	foggy	snow
Tuesday morning:	sunny	cloudy	nice	warm

K WHAT DOES EVERYBODY WANT TO DO TOMORROW?

want to	wants to

1. I _____want to_____ have a picnic tomorrow.

2. George _____ work in his garden.

3. Karen _____ take her children to a concert.

4. Mr. and Mrs. Sato _____ go to the beach.

5. You _____ see a movie.

6. I _____ see a play.

7. My friends _____ go to a basketball game.

L BAD WEATHER

go skiing	go sailing	snow	be cold
take her son to the zoo	go jogging	rain	be warm

1. What does Richard want to do tomorrow?

_____He wants to go sailing._____

What's the forecast?

_____It's going to rain._____

2. What does Lucy want to do this afternoon?

_____

What's the forecast?

_____

3. What do Carl and Betty want to do today?

_____

What's the forecast?

_____

4. What does Jeff want to do tomorrow morning?

_____

What's the forecast?

_____

M YES AND NO

doesn't want to
don't want to

YES!

NO!

1. My parents want to buy a new car. _____They don't want to buy_____ a motorcycle.

2. David wants to go to a baseball game. _____ to a concert.

3. I want to wash my car. _____ my clothes.

4. Nancy and Pam want to play baseball. _____ soccer.

5. Michael wants to cook Italian food. _____ American food.

6. We want to study English. _____ history.

7. Margaret wants to dance with John. _____ with Jim.

8. I want to work in the garden today. _____ in the kitchen.

N YES AND NO

I'm	not	
He She It	isn't	going to
We You They	aren't	

1. Steven is going to go swimming. _____He isn't going to go_____ sailing.

2. I'm going to take a shower. _____ a bath.

3. We're going to go bowling. _____ shopping.

4. Barbara is going to go to the beach. _____ to the mall.

5. My parents are going to clean the attic. _____ the basement.

6. It's going to be warm. _____ cool.

7. Robert is going to listen to the news. _____ the forecast.

8. You're going to buy a used car. _____ a new car.

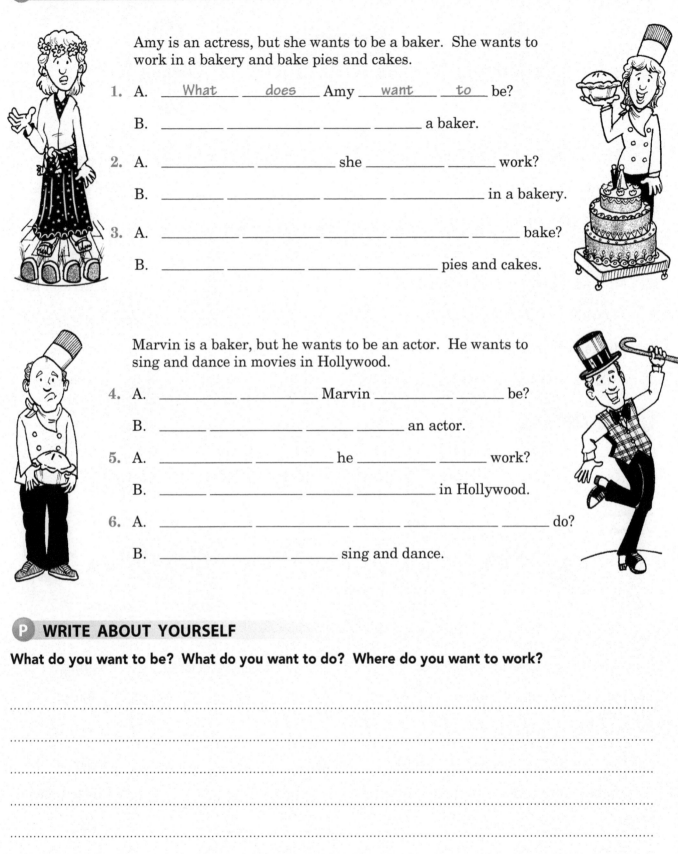

O WHAT DO THEY WANT TO BE?

Amy is an actress, but she wants to be a baker. She wants to work in a bakery and bake pies and cakes.

1. A. ____What____ ____does____ Amy ____want____ ____to____ be?

   B. ____ ____ ____ ____ a baker.

2. A. ____ ____ she ____ ____ work?

   B. ____ ____ ____ ____ in a bakery.

3. A. ____ ____ ____ ____ bake?

   B. ____ ____ ____ ____ pies and cakes.

Marvin is a baker, but he wants to be an actor. He wants to sing and dance in movies in Hollywood.

4. A. ____ ____ Marvin ____ ____ be?

   B. ____ ____ ____ ____ an actor.

5. A. ____ ____ he ____ ____ work?

   B. ____ ____ ____ ____ in Hollywood.

6. A. ____ ____ ____ ____ do?

   B. ____ ____ ____ sing and dance.

P WRITE ABOUT YOURSELF

What do you want to be? What do you want to do? Where do you want to work?

....

....

....

....

....

Q GRAMMARRAP: *What Do They Want to Do?*

Listen. Then clap and practice.

> want to = wanna
> wants to = wantsta

He wants to   go.
I want to   stay.
He wants to   work.
I want to   play.

She wants to   eat at a   restaurant.
I want to   eat at   home.
She wants to   eat with   all our   friends.
I want to   eat   alone.

We want to   leave at   seven.
They want to   leave at   eight.
We want to   get there   early.
They want to   get there   late.

Jack wants to   take the   eight o'clock   plane.
Joe wants to   take the   bus.
Bob wants to   take the   six o'clock   train.
Bill wants to   come with   us.

R WHAT TIME IS IT?

Draw the time on the clocks.

1. It's ten o'clock.   2. It's five fifteen.   3. It's nine thirty.   4. It's three forty-five.

5. It's noon.   6. It's half past eleven.   7. It's a quarter to one.   8. It's a quarter after two.

S WHICH TIMES ARE CORRECT?

Circle the correct times.

1. a. It's four o'clock.
   b. It's five o'clock.

2. a. It's eleven thirteen.
   b. It's eleven thirty.

3. a. It's a quarter after nine.
   b. It's three fifteen.

4. a. It's noon.
   b. It's midnight.

5. a. It's half past six.
   b. It's twelve thirty.

6. a. It's two fifteen.
   b. It's a quarter to three.

7. a. It's one thirty.
   b. It's one forty-five.

8. a. It's a quarter to seven.
   b. It's a quarter after seven.

9. a. It's six o'clock.
   b. It's midnight.

T LISTENING

Listen and write the time you hear.

1.  7:45   4. _____   7. _____   10. _____

2. _____   5. _____   8. _____   11. _____

3. _____   6. _____   9. _____   12. _____

U ALAN CHANG'S DAY

Alan Chang gets up every day at seven fifteen.
He brushes his teeth and takes a shower. At seven
forty-five he eats breakfast and reads his e-mail.
At eight thirty he leaves the house and drives to
work. Alan works at a computer company. He
begins work at nine o'clock. Every day he uses
business software on the computer and talks to
people on the telephone. At twelve o'clock Alan is
always hungry and thirsty. He eats lunch in the
cafeteria. Alan leaves work at five thirty. He eats
dinner at six o'clock and then at half past seven he
watches videos on his new DVD player.

1. What time does Alan get up every day? _____ *He gets up at 7:15.*

2. What time does he eat breakfast? _____

3. What time does he leave the house? _____

4. What time does he begin work? _____

5. Where does Alan work? _____

6. What does he do at noon? _____

7. What does he do at half past five? _____

8. What time does he eat dinner? _____

9. What does he do at seven thirty? _____

V YOUR DAY

Answer in complete sentences.

1. What time do you usually get up? ....

2. What do you do after you get up? ....

3. When do you usually leave for school or work? ....

4. What time do you usually have lunch? ....

5. When do you get home from school or work? ....

6. What time do you usually have dinner? ....

7. What do you usually do after dinner? ....

8. When do you usually go to bed? ....

W GRAMMARRAP: *Time Flies*

Listen. Then clap and practice.

Time   flies.
The days go   by.
    Monday,   Tuesday,
    Wednesday, Thursday,
    Friday,   Saturday.
    Time   flies.
The days go   by.

    Time   flies.
The months go   by.
    January,   February,   March,   April,
    May,   June,   July,   August,
    September, October,   November,   December.
    Time   flies.
The months go   by.

The seasons   come,
The seasons   go.
    Autumn,   winter,   spring,   summer,
    Autumn,   winter,   spring,   summer.
    Time   flies.
The years go   by.
    Where do they   go?
    I don't   know.

GrammarSong: *To Be With You*

Listen and fill in the words to the song. Then listen again and sing along.

I'm	going	be	after	day	year	December	April	right
it's	wait	in	past	month	fall	February	July	
you	waiting	to	with	week	summer	September		

Any day, any ___week___ ¹, any month, any _____ ², I'm _____ _____ ³

wait right here to be with you.

_____ ⁴ the spring, in the _____ ⁵, in the winter, or the _____ ⁶, just call.

I'm _____ ⁷ here to be with you.

_____ _____ ⁸ to wait from January, _____ ⁹ March,

_____ ¹⁰, May, June and _____ ¹¹, August, _____ ¹², October,

and November, and all of _____ ¹³. I'm going to wait . . .

_____ ¹⁴ one o'clock, a quarter _____ ¹⁵. It's half _____ ¹⁶ one, a quarter

_____ ¹⁷ two. And I'm going _____ _____ ¹⁸ right here to be with you.

Any _____ ¹⁹, any week, any _____ ²⁰, any year, I'm going to wait

_____ ²¹ here to be _____ ²² you.

Yes, I'm going to wait right here _____ _____ ²³ with _____ ²⁴.

A.

Ex. Ted _____wants to go skating_____, but

he can't. He _has to fix his car_.

1. We _____, but

_____. We _____.

2. Alice _____, but

_____. She _____.

3. I _____, but

_____. I _____.

B. Fill in the blanks.

is	are	do	does

Ex. When __is__ Harry going to leave the house?

1. When _____ you going to call the mechanic?

2. _____ you have a bad cold?

3. What _____ they going to do this evening?

4. Where _____ you going skiing?

5. What _____ Carol have to do this Tuesday?

6. _____ your son going to take a bath today?

C. *Ex.* Tom wants to move next spring. _____He doesn't want to move_____ this fall.

Dad is going to fix the sink. _____He isn't going to fix_____ the car.

1. I want to teach French. _____ English.

2. We're going to bed at 10:00. _____ at 9:00.

3. Mrs. Miller can bake pies. _____ cakes.

4. Frank has to go to the dentist. _____ the doctor.

5. Jim and Julie can speak Japanese. _____ Spanish.

6. We have to do our homework. _____ our exercises.

D. Every day Helen gets up at 7:30. At 8:00 she eats breakfast, and at 8:30 she goes to work. At noon she has lunch, and at 5:00 she takes the bus home. What's Helen going to do tomorrow?

Tomorrow Helen _____*is going to get up*_____ at 7:30. At 8:00 she's

_____¹ breakfast, and at 8:30 _____² to work. At noon

_____³ lunch, and at 5:00 _____⁴ home.

E. Write the question.

What	When	Where

Ex. I'm going to clean my house <u>this evening</u>.   ____*When are you going to clean your house?*____

1. She's going to <u>fix her sink</u> tomorrow.   _____

2. He's going to play tennis <u>in the park</u>.   _____

3. I'm going to go to the zoo <u>this weekend</u>.   _____

4. They're going to study <u>Spanish</u> next year.   _____

F. What time is it?

Ex.

It's ten o'clock.

1.

It's five fifteen.

2.

It's nine thirty.

3.

It's noon.

4.

It's two forty-five.

5.

It's a quarter after eleven.

G. Listen to the story. Fill in the correct times.

English	_____	Chinese	_____	lunch	_____
mathematics	_____	science	_____	music	_____

A TIME ZONES

Read the article on student book page 139 and answer the questions.

1. How many time zones are there around the world?
   a. Twelve
   b. Twenty
   c. Twenty-four
   d. Twenty-five

2. When it's 3:00 in your time zone, what time is it in the time zone to your east?
   a. 2:00
   b. 4:00
   c. 1:00
   d. 5:00

3. When it's 6:30 in your time zone, what time is it in the time zone to your west?
   a. 7:00
   b. 5:00
   c. 7:30
   d. 5:30

4. What time is it in Los Angeles when it's 11:00 in New York?
   a. 10:00
   b. 9:00
   c. 8:00
   d. 7:00

5. When it's noon in New Zealand, what are people doing in London?
   a. They're sleeping.
   b. They're eating lunch.
   c. They're eating breakfast.
   d. They're eating dinner.

6. Which city is an hour ahead of Chicago?
   a. Los Angeles
   b. Denver
   c. New York
   d. London

7. Which city is two hours behind Chicago?
   a. New York
   b. Los Angeles
   c. Denver
   d. London

8. What time is it in New York when it's 11:00 A.M. in Chicago?
   a. 10:00 A.M.
   b. 1:00 P.M.
   c. Midnight
   d. Noon

STUDENT BOOK
PAGES 139–140

B BUILD YOUR VOCABULARY!

Choose the job that is right for each person.

_____ 1. Alessandro can use a cash register.

_____ 2. Jane wants to work in a restaurant.

_____ 3. George can use tools. He likes to fix things.

_____ 4. Josefina can speak three languages fluently.

_____ 5. Greta likes to work outdoors.

_____ 6. Sally wants to design buildings.

_____ 7. Bianca can fly airplanes.

_____ 8. Vladimir can paint houses.

a. painter
b. translator
c. cashier
d. architect
e. waitress
f. pilot
g. carpenter
h. farmer

C FACT FILE

Look at the Fact File on student book page 139 and answer the questions.

1. When it's 7:00 A.M. in Mexico City, it's 9:00 P.M. in _____.
   a. Caracas
   b. Lisbon
   c. Hong Kong
   d. Moscow

2. When it's 2:00 P.M. in Madrid, it's also 2:00 P.M. in _____.
   a. Istanbul
   b. Lisbon
   c. Buenos Aires
   d. Rome

3. When it's 5:00 A.M. in Los Angeles, people in Lisbon are _____.
   a. having lunch
   b. having breakfast
   c. going to bed
   d. getting up

4. _____ is two hours ahead of London.
   a. Moscow
   b. Athens
   c. Rome
   d. Rio de Janeiro

5. Istanbul is _____ behind Seoul.
   a. three hours
   b. four hours
   c. seven hours
   d. ten hours

6. When it's 3:00 P.M. in Athens, _____ in Sydney, Australia.
   a. it's noon
   b. it's midnight
   c. people are eating breakfast
   d. people are eating lunch

7. _____ are in the same time zone.
   a. Caracas and Rio de Janeiro
   b. Moscow and Istanbul
   c. Paris and Athens
   d. New York City and Toronto

8. When it's 8:00 A.M. in Toronto, _____.
   a. it's 10:00 A.M. in Seoul
   b. it's 1:00 A.M. in London
   c. it's 2:00 P.M. in Paris
   d. it's 3:00 P.M. in Moscow

D "CAN-DO" REVIEW

Match the "can do" statement and the correct sentence.

____ 1. I can tell my occupation.

____ 2. I can ask about a person's skills.

____ 3. I can tell about my skills.

____ 4. I can express my job interests.

____ 5. I can express inability to do something.

____ 6. I can express obligation.

____ 7. I can give the time.

____ 8. I can tell about future plans.

____ 9. I can ask about the weather.

____ 10. I can ask the time.

a. I'm looking for a job as a chef.

b. I have to take a road test.

c. What time is it?

d. I'm a construction worker.

e. I'm going to wash my clothes tomorrow.

f. I can't drive a truck.

g. What's the forecast?

h. I can use business software.

i. It's four o'clock.

j. Can you type?

A WHAT'S THE MATTER?

backache	cough	fever	sore throat	toothache
cold	earache	headache	stomachache	

1. He _____*has a cold*_____

_____.

2. She _____

_____.

3. I _____

_____.

4. She _____

_____.

5. I _____

_____.

6. He _____

_____.

7. She _____

_____.

8. You _____

_____.

9. He _____

_____.

B LISTENING

Listen to the story. Put the number under the correct picture.

_____

___1___

_____

_____

_____

_____

_____

_____

C GRAMMARRAP: *What's the Matter?*

Listen. Then clap and practice.

A. What's the matter with   you?

B. I have a headache.

    What's the matter with   YOU?

A. I have a cold.

A. What's the matter with   him?

B. He has a toothache.

    What's the matter with   HER?

A. She has a cold.

A. What's the matter with   Mary?

B. She has an earache.

    What's the matter with   BILL?

A. He has a very bad   cold.

A. What's the matter with   Fred?

B. He has a backache.

    What's the matter with   ANNE?

A. She has an awful   cold.

A. What's the matter with   Jane?

B. She has a stomachache.

    What's the matter with   PAUL?

A. He has a terrible   cold.

A. What's the matter with the   students?

B. They have sore   throats.

    What's the matter with the   teachers?

A. They have terrible   colds.

    They have terrible   terrible

    colds!

D **WHAT DID YOU DO YESTERDAY?**

bake	cook	dance	rest	shout	study
clean	cry	paint	shave	smile	type

1. I _____cooked_____.

2. I _____.

3. I _____.

4. I _____.

5. I _____.

6. I _____.

7. I _____.

8. I _____.

9. I _____.

10. I _____.

11. I _____.

12. I _____.

E WHAT'S THE WORD?

| brush | cook | paint | plant | play | study | wait | watch | work |

1. I _____work_____ in an office every day.

2. I _____played_____ the guitar yesterday.

3. I _____ my teeth every day.

4. I _____ flowers yesterday.

5. I _____ dinner every day.

6. I _____ English yesterday.

7. I _____ my fence yesterday.

8. I _____ TV every day.

9. I _____ for the bus yesterday.

F LISTENING

Listen and circle the correct answer.

Ex. I study. ~~yesterday~~ (every day)   I played cards. (yesterday) every day

1. yesterday / every day
2. yesterday / every day
3. yesterday / every day
4. yesterday / every day
5. yesterday / every day
6. yesterday / every day
7. yesterday / every day
8. yesterday / every day
9. yesterday / every day
10. yesterday / every day
11. yesterday / every day
12. yesterday / every day

WHAT DID EVERYBODY DO?

| bark | clean | cry | drink | eat | ride | sing | sit | skate | write |

1. A. What did James do today?

   B. _____He cleaned_____ his apartment
   all day.

2. A. What did your sister do today?

   B. _____ letters
   all morning.

3. A. What did Mr. and Mrs. Porter do
   yesterday?

   B. _____ songs
   all evening.

4. A. What did you and your friends do
   today?

   B. _____ in the
   park all afternoon.

5. A. What did Linda do yesterday?

   B. _____ lemonade
   all morning.

6. A. What did Jimmy do today?

   B. _____ candy
   and cookies all day.

7. A. What did Mrs. Mason's children do
   today?

   B. _____ all afternoon.

8. A. What did the neighbors' dogs do
   yesterday?

   B. _____ all night.

9. A. What did Howard do yesterday?

   B. _____ in the clinic
   all evening.

10. A. What did Grandma do today?

    B. _____
    her bicycle all afternoon.

H PUZZLE

Across

3. ride
4. study
6. eat

Down

1. cry
2. work
4. sit
5. drink

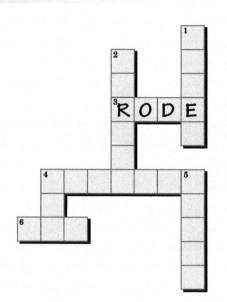

I PETER'S DAY AT HOME

bake	cook	fix	paint	plant	rest	wash

1. Thank you, Peter. This is a very good dinner.

2. This is a wonderful cake, Peter.

3. Look at the car! It's really clean. Thank you.

4. The new flowers in the garden are beautiful.

5. The kitchen looks beautiful. Yellow is my favorite color.

6. The sink isn't broken! I can brush my teeth in the bathroom now!

What did Peter do today?

1. _____He cooked dinner._____   2. _____

3. _____   4. _____

5. _____   6. _____

What did Peter do after dinner?

7. _____

J **GRAMMARRAP:** *What Did They Do?*

Listen. Then clap and practice.

washed [t]	cleaned [d]	painted [ɪd]

A.   What did you   do   today?

B.   I washed my   floors.

A. Your floors?   B.   Yes!

B.   I washed my   floors all   day!

A.   What did Mark   do   today?

B.   He cleaned his   house.

A.   His house?   B.   Yes!

B.   He cleaned his   house all   day!

A.   What did Pam   do   today?

B. She painted her   porch.

A.   Her porch?   B.   Yes!

B. She painted her   porch all   day!

A.   What did they   do   today?

B.   They sang some   songs.

A. Some songs?   B.   Yes!

They sang some   songs all   day!

A.   What did you   do   today?

B.   I _____.

A.   _____?   B.   Yes!

B.   I _____   all day!

K MY GRANDFATHER'S BIRTHDAY PARTY

At my grandfather's birthday party last night, everybody (listen) _____listened_____ ¹ to

Mexican music and (dance) _____ ². My sister Gloria (sing) _____ ³ my

grandfather's favorite songs all evening, and my brother Daniel (play) _____ ⁴ the

guitar.

Everybody (sit) _____ ⁵ in the living room with my grandmother and grandfather

and (look) _____ ⁶ at old photographs. We (laugh) _____ ⁷, we (smile)

_____ ⁸, we (cry) _____ ⁹, and we (talk) _____ ¹⁰ about "the good

old days." What did I do at my grandfather's birthday party? I (drink) _____ ¹¹

lemonade and (eat) _____ ¹² a lot of food!

L MATCHING

_e_	1.	At the party my brother played _____.	a.	drank lemonade all night
____	2.	Everybody sat and talked about _____.	b.	Mexican music
____	3.	My sister has a sore throat today because _____.	c.	"the good old days"
____	4.	We all looked at _____.	d.	ate a lot of food
____	5.	We listened to _____.	e.	the guitar
____	6.	I have a toothache today because I _____.	f.	old photographs
____	7.	I also have a stomachache because I _____.	g.	she sang all evening

1. Jennifer brushed her teeth last night.

_____ *She didn't brush her teeth.* _____

_____ *She brushed her hair.* _____

2. Kevin played the violin yesterday afternoon.

_____

3. Harold and Betty listened to the news yesterday evening.

_____

_____

4. Mrs. Martinez waited for the train this afternoon.

_____

_____

5. Frank fixed his fence yesterday morning.

_____

_____

6. Mr. and Mrs. Park cleaned their attic today.

_____

_____

7. Marvin baked a pie yesterday evening.

_____

_____

8. Patty called her grandmother last night.

_____

_____

B ALAN AND HIS SISTER

Alan and his sister Ellen did very different things yesterday. Alan (rest) _____rested_____ [1] all

day. He didn't (work) _____ [2], and he didn't (study) _____ [3]. He (listen)

_____ [4] to music yesterday morning. He (watch) _____ [5] game shows on TV

yesterday afternoon. And yesterday evening he (talk) _____ [6] to his friends on the

telephone and (play) _____ [7] games on his computer.

Ellen didn't (listen) _____ [8] to music. She didn't (watch) _____ [9] game shows on

TV, and she didn't (play) _____ [10] games on her computer. What did she do? She (study)

_____ [11] English yesterday morning. She (clean) _____ [12] the yard yesterday

afternoon. And she (cook) _____ [13] dinner for her family last night.

C YES AND NO

1. Did Alan rest all day yesterday?   _____Yes, he did._____

2. Did Ellen rest all day yesterday?   _____No, she didn't._____

3. Did Ellen study yesterday morning?   _____

4. Did Alan study yesterday morning?   _____

5. Did Alan watch TV yesterday afternoon?   _____

6. _____Did Ellen clean_____ the yard yesterday afternoon?   Yes, she did.

7. _____ to his friends yesterday evening?   Yes, he did.

8. _____ dinner for his family last night?   No, he didn't.

9. _____ to music yesterday morning?   No, she didn't.

10. _____ game shows yesterday afternoon?   No, she didn't.

11. _____ English yesterday afternoon?   No, he didn't.

D WHAT DID THEY DO?

1. I didn't buy a car. I ____bought____ a motorcycle.

2. Michael didn't have a headache. He _____ a toothache.

3. Alice didn't write to her uncle. She _____ to her cousin.

4. We didn't do our homework last night. We _____ yoga.

5. They didn't take the bus to work today. They _____ the train.

6. Barbara didn't get up at 7:00 this morning. She _____ up at 6:00.

7. My friend and I didn't go swimming yesterday. We _____ bowling.

8. Martha didn't read the newspaper last night. She _____ a book.

9. My children didn't make breakfast this morning. They _____ lunch.

E THEY DIDN'T DO WHAT THEY USUALLY DO

1. Robert usually writes to his friends.

    He __didn't__ __write__ to his friends yesterday.

    He __wrote__ to his grandparents.

2. I usually have a cold in January.

    I _____ _____ a cold last January.

    I _____ a cold last July.

3. We usually eat at home on Friday night.

    We _____ _____ at home last Friday night.

    We _____ at a very nice restaurant.

4. Bill usually gets up 7:00 o'clock.

    He _____ _____ up at 7:00 this morning.

    He _____ up at 10:00.

5. Tom and Tina usually go dancing every week.

    They _____ _____ dancing this week.

    They _____ sailing.

6. Susie usually drinks milk every afternoon.

    She _____ _____ milk this afternoon.

    She _____ lemonade.

7. My brother usually makes lunch on Sunday.

    He _____ _____ lunch last Sunday.

    He _____ dinner.

8. Mr. Lee usually takes his wife to the movies.

    He _____ _____ his wife to the movies last night.

    He _____ his daughter and his son-in-law.

9. We usually buy food at a large supermarket.

    We _____ _____ food at a supermarket today.

    We _____ food at a small grocery store.

10. I usually sit next to Maria in English class.

    I _____ _____ next to Maria yesterday.

    I _____ next to her sister Carmen.

A.   Did she wash her   skirt?

B.   No, she   didn't.

A.   What did she   wash?

B.   She washed her <u> shirt </u>.

A.   Did they paint the   door?

B.   No, they   didn't.

A.   What did they paint?

B.   They painted the _____.

A.   Did he call his   mother?

B.   No, he   didn't.

A.   Who did he   call?

B.   He called his _____.

A.   Did you buy   new suits?

B.   No, we   didn't.

A.   What did you   buy?

B.   We bought new _____.

A.   Did you get up at   seven?

B.   No, I   didn't.

A.   When did you get   up?

B.   I got up at   _____.

G WHAT'S THE ANSWER?

1. Did Henry ride his bicycle to work this morning?   Yes, _____he did_____.

2. Did you get up at 6:00 this morning?   No, _____.

3. Did your sister call you last night?   Yes, _____.

4. Did Mr. and Mrs. Chen clean their apartment last weekend?   No, _____.

5. Did you and your friends go to the library yesterday afternoon?   Yes, _____.

6. Did your father make spaghetti for dinner last night?   No, _____.

7. Excuse me. Did I take your gloves?   Yes, _____.

8. Bob, did you do your exercises today?   No, _____.

H WHAT'S THE QUESTION?

1. _____Did she buy_____ a car?   No, she didn't. She bought a truck.

2. _____ a headache?   No, he didn't. He had a backache.

3. _____ a shower?   No, I didn't. I took a bath.

4. _____ to the supermarket?   No, they didn't. They went to the bank.

5. _____ in the living room?   No, we didn't. We sat in the kitchen.

6. _____ a right turn?   No, you didn't. You made a left turn.

I LISTENING

Listen and choose the correct response.

1. a. I write to her every day.
   b. I wrote to her this morning. *(circled)*

2. a. He washes it every weekend.
   b. He washed it last weekend.

3. a. They visit my aunt and my uncle.
   b. They visited my aunt and my uncle.

4. a. She did yoga in the park.
   b. She does yoga in the park.

5. a. He went to sleep at 8:00.
   b. He goes to sleep at 8:00.

6. a. We clean it every weekend.
   b. We cleaned it last weekend.

7. a. We take them to the zoo.
   b. We took them to the zoo.

8. a. I make spaghetti.
   b. I made spaghetti.

9. a. She reads it every afternoon.
   b. She read it this afternoon.

10. a. I get up at 7:00.
    b. I got up at 7:00.

J I'M SORRY I'M LATE!

forget	go	have to	miss
get up	have	meet	steal

1. I _____missed_____ the train.

3. I _____ my lunch.

5. I _____ late.

7. I _____ go
to the bank.

2. I _____ a headache.

4. I _____ my girlfriend
on the way to work.

6. A thief _____ my bicycle.

8. I _____ to sleep
on the bus.

K MATCHING

_d_ 1. buy   a. wrote

____ 2. steal   b. did

____ 3. do   c. went

____ 4. see   d. bought

____ 5. go   e. saw

____ 6. write   f. stole

____ 7. get   g. had

____ 8. eat   h. drove

____ 9. have   i. made

____ 10. forget   j. got

____ 11. make   k. forgot

____ 12. drive   l. ate

GRAMMARRAP: *Old Friends*

Listen. Then clap and practice.

We walked and   talked

And talked and   walked.

Walked and   talked,

Talked and   walked.

We sat in the   garden

And looked at the   flowers.

We talked and   talked

For hours and   hours.

He drank   milk,

And I drank   tea.

We talked and   talked

From one to   three.

We talked about him.

We talked about us.

Then we walked to the corner

To get the   bus.

We waited and   waited.

The bus was   late.

So we stood and   talked

From four to   eight.

M **GRAMMARRAP:** *Gossip*

Listen. Then clap and practice.

I told   Jack.

Jack told   Jill.

Jill told   Fred.

Fred told   Bill.

Bill called   Anne.

Anne called   Sue.

Sue told   Jim.

But who told   you?

A A TERRIBLE DAY AND A WONDERFUL DAY

| was | were |

We _____ were _____ ¹ very upset at work last Friday. Our

computers _____ ² broken, our boss _____ ³ angry

because he _____ ⁴ tired, and my friends and I

_____ ⁵ sick. Outside it _____ ⁶ cloudy and it

_____ ⁷ very cold. And then in the afternoon all the

trains _____ ⁸ late. I _____ ⁹ hungry when I

got home, and my children _____ ¹⁰ very noisy. It

_____ ¹¹ a terrible day!

We _____ were _____ ¹² very happy at work on Monday. Our

computers _____ ¹³ fine, our boss _____ ¹⁴ happy,

and my friends and I _____ ¹⁵ energetic. Outside it

_____ ¹⁶ sunny, it _____ ¹⁷ warm, and all the trains

_____ ¹⁸ early. My children _____ ¹⁹ very quiet

when I got home. We ate a big dinner, and I _____ ²⁰ very

full. It was a wonderful day!

B LISTENING

Listen and circle the word you hear.

1.	(is) / was	4.	is / was	7.	are / were	10.	is / was
2.	is / was	5.	is / was	8.	are / were	11.	are / were
3.	are / were	6.	are / were	9.	is / was	12.	are / were

Activity Workbook   129

clean	enormous	happy	shiny	thin
comfortable	full	healthy	tall	

1. Before I took A-1 Vitamins, I ___was___ always
   sick. Now __I'm__ __healthy__.

2. Before Harold met Gertrude, he _____ sad.
   Now _____ _____ all the time.

3. Before we ate a big breakfast today, we _____
   hungry. Now _____ _____.

4. Before Helen got her new sofa, she _____
   uncomfortable. Now _____ very _____.

5. Before you drank A-1 Skim Milk, you _____
   heavy. Now _____ _____.

6. Before Charlie used A-1 Car Wax, his car _____
   dull. Now _____ _____.

7. Before these children used A-1 soap, they
   _____ dirty. Now _____ _____.

8. When I _____ young, I _____ very short.
   Now _____ _____.

9. Before we bought A-1 Bird Food, our birds _____
   very tiny. Now _____ _____.

D WHAT'S THE WORD?

1. A. _____Were_____ you at a concert last night?

   B. No, I ___wasn't___. I ___was___ at a play.

3. A. _____ your boss in the office yesterday?

   B. No, she _____. She _____ on vacation.

5. A. _____ the questions on the examination easy?

   B. No, they _____. They _____ very difficult.

2. A. _____ your neighbors quiet last Saturday night?

   B. No, they _____. They _____ very noisy.

4. A. _____ we at home last Tuesday?

   B. No, we _____. We _____ at the mall.

6. A. _____ Timothy on time for his wedding?

   B. No, he _____. He _____ late.

E LISTENING

Listen and circle the word you hear.

1. was
   (wasn't)

2. were
   weren't

3. were
   weren't

4. was
   wasn't

5. was
   wasn't

6. were
   weren't

7. were
   weren't

8. was
   wasn't

F **WHAT'S THE WORD?**

did	was	were
didn't	wasn't	weren't

A. Why _____did_____ [1] Victor leave the party early?

B. He _____ [2] like the party. It _____ [3] noisy, the food _____ [4] very good, and his friends _____ [5] there.

A. Where _____ [6] you last week? You _____ [7] at work.

B. That's right. I _____ [8].

A. _____ [9] you sick?

B. Yes, I _____ [10]. I _____ [11] very sick. I had an earache and a cold.

A. _____ [12] you also have a headache?

B. No. I _____ [13] have a headache, but I had a sore throat. I _____ [14] go to work all week. I _____ [15] really sick!

A. How _____ [16] your vacation?

B. It _____ [17] terrible!

A. That's too bad. _____ [18] you like the hotel?

B. No, we _____ [19]. The bathroom sink _____ [20] broken, the hotel room _____ [21] clean, and we _____ [22] sleep well at night because the people in the next room _____ [23] very loud.

A. _____ [24] you swim at the beach?

B. No, we _____ [25]. The weather _____ [26] very cold!

A. _____ [27] your grandchildren visit you last weekend?

B. No, they _____ [28].

A. That's too bad. _____ [29] they busy?

B. My grandson _____ [30] feel well, and my granddaughter _____ [31] on a business trip. We _____ [32] sad because we _____ [33] see them.

Listen. Then clap and practice.

A.   Were you late this   morning?

B.   No, I wasn't. I was   early.

A.   Was he sick last   night?

B.   No, he wasn't. He was   fine.

A.   Was her hair very   straight?

B.   No, it wasn't. It was   curly.

A.   Were there eight new   lessons?

B.   No, there weren't. There were nine.

A.   Was the movie   short?

B.   No, it wasn't. It was   long.

A.   Was the food   expensive?

B.   No, it wasn't. It was   free.

A.   Was I right?

B.   No, you weren't. You were   wrong.

A.   Were the tickets two   dollars?

B.   No, they weren't. They were three.

H WHAT ARE THEY SAYING?

basketball	did	freckles	short	subjects	wasn't	weren't
curly	didn't	hobby	sports	was	were	

A. Tell me, what ____did____ ¹ you look like when you _____ ² young? _____ ³ you tall?

B. No, I _____ ⁴. I _____ ⁵ _____ ⁶.

A. _____ ⁷ you have straight hair?

B. No, I _____ ⁸. I had _____ ⁹ hair.

A. Oh. And _____ ¹⁰ you have dimples?

B. No, I _____ ¹¹, but I had _____ ¹².

A. I'm sure you _____ ¹³ very cute!

   What _____ ¹⁴ you do with your friends?

B. We played sports.

A. Oh. What _____ ¹⁵ you play?

B. We played _____ ¹⁶ and tennis.

A. Tell me, _____ ¹⁷ you like school?

B. Yes. I liked school a lot.

A. What _____ ¹⁸ your favorite _____ ¹⁹?

B. English and mathematics.

A. _____ ²⁰ you have a _____ ²¹?

B. Yes, I _____ ²². I played chess.

I LISTENING

Listen and choose the correct response.

1. a. I was born last week.
   b. I was born in Japan. *(b circled)*

2. a. Yes, I did.
   b. I grew up in Tokyo.

3. a. English.
   b. No, I didn't.

4. a. In Los Angeles.
   b. Last year.

5. a. I was tall and thin.
   b. I didn't look.

6. a. No. I had straight hair.
   b. No. I had dimples.

7. a. I played sports.
   b. I play chess.

8. a. Yes. I'm here.
   b. Yes. My father.

GRAMMARRAP: *The Teacher Was There*

Listen. Then clap and practice.

A.   The teacher was   there,

    But where were the   students?

B.   The students were   there.

All.   Where?

A.   The teacher was   there,

    The students were   there,

    But where were the   books?

B.   The books were   there.

All.   Where?

A.   The teacher was   there,

    The students were   there,

    The books were   there,

    But where was the   chalk?

B.   The chalk was   there.

All.   Where?

A.   The teacher was   there,

    The students were   there,

    The books were   there,

    The chalk was   there,

    But where were the   chairs?

B.   The chairs were   there.

All.   Where?

B.   There.

All.   Where?

B.   Right there!

    Right   there!

A. Fill in the blanks.

was	were	wasn't	weren't

1. A. ___Was___ Barbara at work yesterday?

   B. No, she _____. She _____ sick.

2. A. Why _____ you late today?

   B. I _____ late because I _____ on time for the bus.

3. A. Where _____ Grandma and Grandpa last night? They _____ at home.

   B. They _____ at a concert.

B. Complete the sentences.

Ex. Before we washed our car, it ___was___ dirty. Now ___it's___ ___clean___.

1. Before I ate dinner, I _____ hungry. Now _____ _____.

2. When I got my cats, they _____ tiny. Now _____ _____.

3. When we _____ in college, we _____ thin. Now _____ _____.

4. When I was young, I _____ energetic. Now _____ _____.

C. Complete the sentences.

Ex. a. Carla usually studies English.
   She ___didn't___ ___study___ English yesterday.
   She ___studied___ mathematics.

   b. Paul usually writes to his friends.
   He ___didn't___ ___write___ to his friends yesterday.
   He ___wrote___ to his cousins.

1. I usually drive to the park on Saturday.
   I _____ _____ to the park last Saturday.
   I _____ to the mall.

2. We usually arrive late.
   We _____ _____ late today.
   We _____ on time.

3. My husband and my son usually shave in the morning.
   They _____ _____ in the morning today.
   They _____ in the afternoon.

4. Bob usually goes jogging in the evening.
   He _____ _____ jogging yesterday evening.
   He _____ dancing.

5. Margaret usually reads the newspaper in the morning.
   She _____ _____ the newspaper yesterday morning.
   She _____ a magazine.

D. Write the question.

Ex. _____Did they get up_____ at 8:00?   No, they didn't. They got up at 10:00.

1. _____ his brother?   No, he didn't. He met his sister.

2. _____ her bicycle?   No, she didn't. She rode her motorcycle.

3. _____ a good time?   No, we didn't. We had a terrible time.

4. _____ lunch?   No, they didn't. They made dinner.

5. _____ a movie?   No, I didn't. I saw a play.

E. Read the story and then write about yesterday.

Every morning I get up early. I brush my teeth, and I do my exercises. Then I sit in the kitchen and I eat breakfast. At 8:00 I go to work. I walk to the drug store and I buy a newspaper. Then I take the train to my office. I don't take the bus, and I don't drive my car.

Yesterday I _____got up_____ early. I _____[1] my teeth, and I _____[2] my exercises. Then I _____[3] in the kitchen and I _____[4] breakfast. At 8:00 I _____[5] to work. I _____[6] to the drug store and I _____[7] a newspaper. Then I _____[8] the train to my office. I _____ _____[9] the bus, and I _____ _____[10] my car.

F. Listen and circle the word you hear.

Ex. (is)
     was

1.   is
     was

2.   are
     were

3.   is
     was

4.   are
     were

5.   is
     was

6.   are
     were

7.   is
     was

8.   are
     were

A ADVERTISEMENTS

Read the article on student book page 165 and answer the questions.

1. You can hear advertisements
   _____.
   a. on top of taxis
   b. in newspapers
   c. on the radio
   d. in magazines

2. An unusual place for an
   advertisement is _____.
   a. on a bus
   b. in an elevator
   c. in the mail
   d. on the Internet

3. You can find advertisements
   everywhere because advertisers
   want to _____.
   a. make products
   b. buy products
   c. sell products
   d. use products

4. The main idea of the article is
   _____.
   a. advertisements are a problem
   b. advertisements are unusual
   c. advertisements are interesting
   d. advertisements are everywhere

5. The article does NOT talk about
   advertisements in _____.
   a. movie theaters
   b. shopping malls
   c. public bathrooms
   d. the sky

6. You often see advertisements on
   billboards when you are _____.
   a. reading the mail
   b. driving on the highway
   c. shopping at the supermarket
   d. looking at a magazine

B BUILD YOUR VOCABULARY! What's the Word?

Write the correct word.

closed	dark	fast	high	light	long	messy	plain	wet

1. Clean your room! It's very _____. There are papers everywhere.

2. Roland was out in the rain all afternoon. His clothes are very _____.

3. The library is open on weekdays, but it's _____ on weekends.

4. At midnight it's very _____ outside.

5. I can carry the sign. It's very _____.

6. I have to go to the barber. My hair is very _____.

7. Alicia always finishes her work before the other students. She's very _____.

8. I can't see the house because there's a very _____ wall in front of it.

9. I don't want a dress with flowers on it. I'm looking for something _____.

C BUILD YOUR VOCABULARY! Crossword

Across

3. The store isn't closed. It's _____.

4. Their fence isn't high. It's _____.

5. Her blouse isn't plain. It's _____.

7. His hair isn't long. It's _____.

Down

1. Our car isn't fast. It's _____.

2. That suitcase isn't light. It's _____.

6. My room isn't messy. It's _____

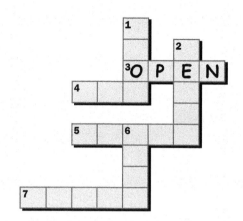

D FACT FILE

Look at the Fact File on student book page 165. Write the countries in alphabetical order.

Australia, _____

_____

E "CAN-DO" REVIEW

Match the "can do" statement and the correct sentence.

____ 1. I can describe my health.

____ 2. I can ask about a person's health.

____ 3. I can ask about past activities.

____ 4. I can tell about past activities.

____ 5. I can apologize for something.

____ 6. I can tell about obligation.

____ 7. I can describe my feelings and emotions.

____ 8. I can express sympathy.

____ 9. I can ask for a recommendation.

____ 10. I can give a recommendation.

a. I have to do my homework.

b. What did you do yesterday?

c. I was happy.

d. I recommend *Presto* Floor Wax.

e. I have a fever.

f. Can you recommend a good restaurant?

g. I'm sorry I'm late.

h. How do you feel today?

i. I'm sorry to hear that.

j. I washed my car yesterday.

A PERSONAL INFORMATION FORM

Fill out the form with your personal information.

LAST NAME   FIRST NAME   MIDDLE INITIAL

NUMBER   STREET   APT. #

CITY   STATE   ZIP CODE

B IDENTIFICATION CARDS

Look at these I.D.s and complete the sentences.

PERMANENT RESIDENT CARD

NAME   Gomez, Gloria M.

INS A#   A92475816

Birthdate   Category   Sex
02/03/97   1RG   F

Country of Birth
Mexico

CARD EXPIRES   11/09/20

Resident Since   04/14/10

```
C1USA0924758166EAC0013440673<<
6003029M1004268MEX<<<<<<<<<<0
SANTOS<<GLORIA<<<<<<<<<<<<<<<<<
```

1. My first name is _____.

2. My last name is _____.

3. My middle initial is _____.

4. I'm from _____.

CALIFORNIA

DMW   DMW

DRIVER LICENSE

Karim Massoud
339 Lake Avenue, Apt. 2A
Los Angeles, CA 90013

Date of Birth: 5/21/93
Issue: 07/09/18

SEX: **HAIR:**   **EYES:**
Male   Brown   Brown
Height: **WEIGHT:**
5-10   175

5. My city is _____.

6. My state is _____.

7. My zip code is _____.

8. My apartment number is _____.

C ADDRESS ABBREVIATIONS

Write the full words next to the abbreviations.

Apartment	Boulevard	North	Street
Avenue	East	South	West

1. Apt. _____
2. N. _____
3. E. _____
4. Blvd. _____

5. Ave. _____
6. S. _____
7. St. _____
8. W. _____

D WRITING ADDRESSES

Write the addresses. Use abbreviations.

1. 31 South Shore Street _____

2. 42 East Central Avenue _____

3. 99 West Lake Boulevard _____

4. 20 North Main Street, Apartment 8A _____

5. 128 South Pond Avenue, Apartment 2B _____

E NUMERACY: Numbers & Words

Choose the correct number.

1. twenty-six (26   36)
2. seventy (70   17)
3. fifty-two (42   52)
4. ninety-three (39   93)

5. sixty-one (51   61)
6. thirty-six (36   46)
7. eighty-two (72   82)
8. forty-five (45   54)

F NUMERACY: Numbers & Words

Write the number.

275	356	418	442	533	612

1. four hundred eighteen _____
2. two hundred seventy-five _____
3. five hundred thirty-three _____

4. six hundred twelve _____
5. four hundred forty-two _____
6. three hundred fifty-six _____

A CLASSROOM INSTRUCTIONS

Complete the sentence with the correct word.

Give	Put	Sit	Take
Go	Raise	Stand	Write

1. _____ out your book.

2. _____ away your book.

3. _____ to the board.

4. _____ your name.

5. _____ down.

6. _____ up.

7. _____ your hand.

8. _____ me your notebook.

B CLASSROOM INSTRUCTIONS: Opposites

Match the opposite classroom instructions.

_____ 1. Stand up.

_____ 2. Write on the board.

_____ 3. Take out your book.

_____ 4. Open your book.

a. Erase the board.

b. Close your book.

c. Sit down.

d. Put away your book.

C NUMERACY: Adding Objects

Choose the correct answer.

1. five pencils + two pencils = (eight   seven) pencils

2. six pens + five pens = (eleven   twelve) pens

3. nine rulers + four rulers = (fifteen   thirteen) rulers

4. sixteen books + seven books = (twenty-two   twenty-three) books

5. thirty chairs + twenty chairs = (fifty   forty) chairs

D NUMERACY: Word Problems with Addition

Solve the word problems.

1. There are four books on the table and twenty-five books on the bookshelf. How many books are there?
   a. twenty-seven
   b. twenty-eight
   c. twenty-nine

2. There are five notebooks on the table and sixteen notebooks on the desks. How many notebooks are there?
   a. twenty-one
   b. twenty-two
   c. twenty-three

3. There are twelve chairs in Room 120 and thirteen chairs in Room 122. How many chairs are there?
   a. fifteen
   b. twenty-five
   c. fifty

4. There are twenty-one desks in Room 301 and nineteen desks in Room 302. How many desks are there?
   a. thirty
   b. forty
   c. forty-one

E CONTINENTS AND COUNTRIES

Write the names of the seven continents on the map.

Africa	Asia	Europe	South America
Antarctica	Australia	North America	

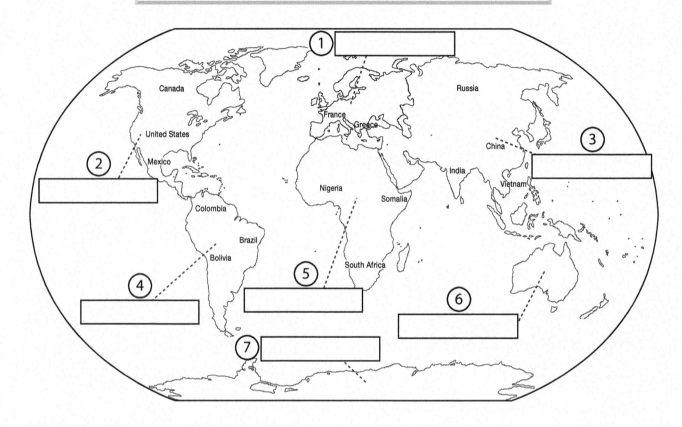

F COUNTRIES AND CONTINENTS

Write the names of the countries in the chart.

Bolivia	China	Greece	Nigeria	South Africa
Brazil	Colombia	India	Russia	United States
Canada	France	Mexico	Somalia	Vietnam

Africa	Asia	Europe	North America	South America
Nigeria	China	France	Canada	Bolivia

A CALLING DIRECTORY ASSISTANCE

Put the conversation in the correct order.

____ Say the name of the business you want, or say, "Residence."

____ James Wilson.

__1__ 411 Directory Assistance. City and state, please.

____ The number is area code (813) 555–2323.

____ Tampa, Florida.

____ Okay. For a residence, say just the person's first and last name.

____ Residence.

B NUMERACY: Reading Telephone Numbers in a Directory

Look at this page from a telephone directory. Choose the correct answer.

Carlson Amy 52 Grove St 478-3296	**Carney Edward** 121 Elm St................................793-2478
Bill 151 Milk St................................. 392-9701	**Nancy** 36 Winter St. 478-1836
Carol 23 Park Ave.............................478-5783	**Carter Anna** 460 8th Ave...............................392-2559
Davor 19 Ellis Rd 793-0065	**Charles** 92 Clifton St...............................793-5741
Erica 825 Queens Blvd.........................392-6735	**Doris** 329 Center St...............................392-6380
Harold 86 17th St................................. 478-6163	**Ella** 521 7th Ave................................478-4195
Ken 190 Western Ave 392-5218	**Irene** 287 Oak Ave................................478-0864
Mary 32 Water St 793-2804	**James** 419 Central Ave..............................793-2217
Rex 466 5th Ave.............................392-1306	**Lisa** 248 8th Ave................................478-8983
Sarah 94 Carter Rd 478-2854	**Casper George** 289 10th Ave............................392-6722

1. Sarah Carlson's phone number is ____.
    a. 478-0864
    b. 478-6163
    c. 478-8983
    d. 478-2854

2. Charles Carter's address is ____.
    a. 23 Park Avenue
    b. 460 Eighth Avenue
    c. 92 Clifton Street
    d. 94 Carter Road

3. Four hundred nineteen Central Avenue is the address of ____.
    a. Doris Carter
    b. James Carter
    c. Anna Carter
    d. Rex Carlson

4. Eighty-six Seventeenth Street is the address of ____.
    a. Carol Carlson
    b. Ella Carter
    c. Harold Carlson
    d. Nancy Carney

5. 248 Eighth Avenue is the address of ____.
    a. Anna Carter
    b. Lisa Carter
    c. Irene Carter
    d. Erica Carlson

6. The phone number of the Carlson at thirty-two Water Street is ____.
    a. 793-2804
    b. 478-1836
    c. 392-5218
    d. 478-5783

7. There are ____ phone numbers for the last name Carlson.
    a. seven
    b. eight
    c. nine
    d. ten

8. 392-5218 is the phone number of ____.
    a. Anna Carter
    b. Ken Carlson
    c. Doris Carter
    d. George Casper

COMMUNITY SERVICE DAY

Circle the words you see in the picture.

brushing	cooking	fixing	planting	reading	teaching
cleaning	feeding	painting	playing	studying	washing

Now complete this story about the picture.

Today is Community Service Day. Students at Center City High School are doing something

to help their school. Asako and Marie are _____ [1] a car. Carlos and John are

_____ [2] around the school. Carmen is _____ [3] the door to the school.

Andrew is _____ [4] a window. Amy and Marc are _____ [5] flowers.

NUMERACY: Word Problems with Addition

Read the story and answer the questions.

It's a busy day for the students at Jackson High School. The sixteen students in Room 102 are studying English. The thirteen students in Room 103 are studying mathematics. The fifteen students in Ms. Lopez's class and the twenty students in Mr. Grant's class are eating lunch in the cafeteria.

Other students are helping in the community because it's Community Service Day. Mr. Rogers and his fourteen students are at the library. They're washing windows. Miss Sinclair and her eleven students are also at the library. They're painting the bookshelves.

The eleven students in Ms. Ali's class and the twelve students in Mr. Benton's class are planting flowers in the park. The fourteen students in Mr. Gallo's class and the nineteen students in Ms. Winter's class are cleaning around the hospital.

The twenty-three students in Ms. Mendoza's class and the eighteen students in Ms. Hamilton's class are washing cars in the school parking lot. They're getting five dollars for every car. The money is for new books for the school library.

1. How many students are studying in their classrooms?
   a. nineteen
   b. twenty-eight
   c. twenty-nine
   d. ninety

2. How many students are eating lunch?
   a. twenty-five
   b. thirty-five
   c. forty-five
   d. fifty-five

3. How many students are planting flowers?
   a. thirteen
   b. twenty-one
   c. twenty-two
   d. twenty-three

4. How many students are washing cars?
   a. forty-one
   b. forty-two
   c. fifty-one
   d. fifty-two

5. How many students are cleaning around the hospital?
   a. thirty-one
   b. thirty-two
   c. thirty-three
   d. thirty-four

6. How many students and teachers are working at the library?
   a. twenty-four
   b. twenty-five
   c. twenty-six
   d. twenty-seven

A **READING A WEATHER MAP**

Read the map and answer the questions.

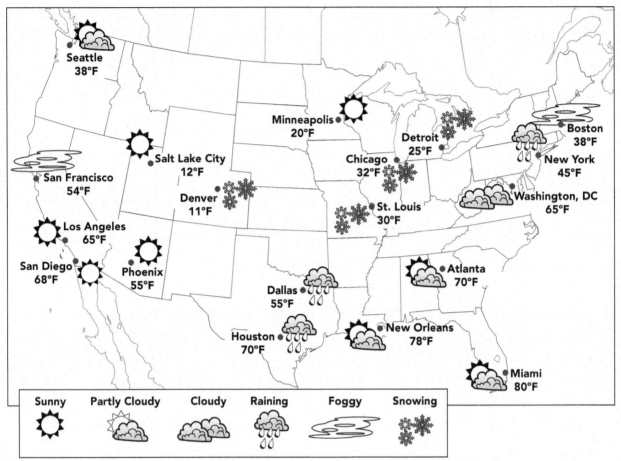

1. What's the weather in San Francisco?
   It's _____.

2. What's the temperature in San Diego?
   It's _____° Fahrenheit.

3. What's the weather in Los Angeles?
   It's _____.

4. What's the temperature in Salt Lake City?
   It's _____° Fahrenheit.

5. What's the temperature in Denver?
   It's _____° Fahrenheit.

6. What's the weather in Washington, DC?
   It's _____.

7. What's the temperature in Dallas?
   It's _____° Fahrenheit.

8. What's the weather in Chicago?
   It's _____.

9. What's the temperature in Miami?
   It's _____° Fahrenheit.

10. What's the weather in Atlanta?
    It's _____.

11. What's the weather in New York?
    It's _____.

12. What's the weather in Boston?
    It's _____.

● **146**   **Activity Workbook**

NUMERACY: Reading a Thermometer

Circle the correct temperature.

1. 50° F
   40° F

2. 15° C
   10° C

3. 95° F
   35° F

4. 35° C
   25° C

5. 55° F
   70° F

6. 21° C
   31° C

C **NUMERACY: Fahrenheit & Celsius Temperatures**

Match the temperatures.

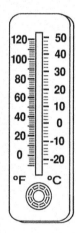

_c_ 1. 32° F   a. 15° C

___ 2. 59° F   b. 25° C

___ 3. 77° F   c. 0° C

___ 4. 68° F   d. 5° C

___ 5. 86° F   e. 20° C

___ 6. 41° F   f. 30° C

D **NUMERACY: Interpreting a Bar Graph**

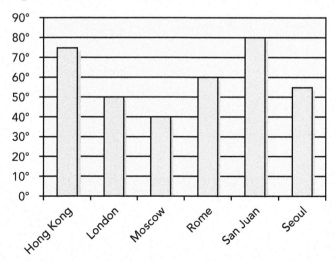

This graph shows the average temperature in Fahrenheit in six cities. Write the name of the city next to its average temperature.

1. 50° F _____

2. 80° F _____

3. 75° F _____

4. 40° F _____

5. 55° F _____

6. 60° F _____

A FAMILY TREE

**Read the story about Jim Smith's family. Complete his family tree
with the correct names.**

Jim Smith's Family

Jim has a big family. He's married to Sandra. They have two children.
Their daughter's name is Lisa, and their son's name is Peter. Jim's parents
are Judy and Michael. His grandmother is Jane and his grandfather is Will.
Jim also has one aunt. Her name is Mary. Jim's sister is Ann. She's single.
Jim's brother is Bob. He's married to Julie. Bob and Julie have two children.
Jim's niece is Amanda and his nephew is Tom.

Jim Smith's Family Tree

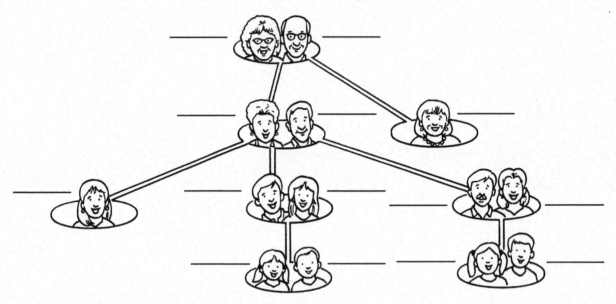

Look at Jim Smith's family tree. Complete the sentences.

1. Michael is Judy's _____.

2. Sandra is Jim's _____.

3. Bob is Peter and Lisa's _____.

4. Ann is Tom and Amanda's _____.

5. Bob is Jim's _____.

6. Mary is Michael's _____.

7. Jane and Will are Ann, Jim, and Bob's _____.

8. Tom and Amanda are Peter and Lisa's _____.

B NUMERACY: Adding Quantities

Write the correct answer in words.

1. one mother + one father = _____ parents

2. two grandfathers + two grandmothers = _____ grandparents

3. one son + two daughters = _____ children

4. three granddaughters + two grandsons = _____ grandchildren

5. five neighbors in Apartment 2 and seven neighbors in Apartment 3 = _____ neighbors

C NUMERACY: Word Problems with Addition

Solve the word problems.

1. Gregory is having a birthday party. He's inviting his two grandmothers, his grandfather, his mother and father, his sister and brother, his favorite aunt and uncle and their three children. He's inviting _____ family members.
   a. ten
   b. eleven
   c. twelve
   d. thirteen

2. Gregory is also inviting eleven friends to his party. He's inviting a total of _____ family members and friends to the party.
   a. twenty-three
   b. thirty-one
   c. thirty-two
   d. thirty-four

3. Chantal is from Haiti. Now she's living in Miami with her grandmother, mother, two brothers, and three sisters. Her father and his parents are in Haiti, but six other family members are in the United States. Chantal and _____ other people in her family are in the United States.
   a. eleven
   b. twelve
   c. thirteen
   d. fourteen

4. Rachel and Marcos are getting married. She's inviting forty-two people in her family to the wedding. She's also inviting eighteen friends. Marcos is inviting thirty-five people in his family and twenty-five friends. Rachel and Marcos are inviting _____ people to their wedding.
   a. one hundred
   b. one hundred ten
   c. one hundred twenty
   d. one hundred thirty

5. Roberta's mother has three sisters and three brothers. Her father has one sister and four brothers. Roberta has _____.
   a. three aunts and six uncles
   b. four aunts and seven uncles
   c. five aunts and five uncles
   d. four aunts and six uncles

6. Jeffrey has four sisters. One sister has one daughter, one sister has two daughters, one sister has three daughters and a son, and one sister has four daughters and two sons. Jeffrey has _____ nieces.
   a. three
   b. eight
   c. nine
   d. ten

A CLASSIFIED AD ABBREVIATIONS

Write the full words next to the abbreviations.

| air conditioning | bathroom | elevator | kitchen | living room |
| apartment | bedroom | garage | large | near |

1. apt. _____
2. gar. _____
3. kit. _____
4. BR _____
5. lge. _____

6. AC _____
7. liv. rm. _____
8. nr. _____
9. elev. _____
10. BA _____

B READING CLASSIFIED ADS

Read the apartment ads. Choose the correct answers.

APT FOR RENT
Westville. Lge. 3 BR, 2 BA apt., lge. kit., AC, washing machine, elev., nr. supermarket & bus station. $1600. Call (529) 335–6359.

APT FOR RENT
Easton. Sunny 2 BR, 1 BA, liv. rm., din. rm., stove & refrigerator in kit., gar., nr. bus stop & shopping mall. $1300. Call (592) 335–3569.

1. There are (three   two) bedrooms in the apartment in Westville.
2. There (is   isn't) a dining room in the apartment in Easton.
3. There (is   isn't) an elevator in the apartment building in Easton.
4. There (is   isn't) air conditioning in the apartment in Westville.
5. The apartment in Easton is near a bus (station   stop).
6. The apartment in Westville is near a (shopping mall   supermarket).
7. The rent for the apartment in Easton is ($1600 $1300).
8. There's a (garage   washing machine) in the apartment building in Easton.
9. Call (592) 335-3569 for the apartment with (an elevator   a stove).

C NUMERACY: Word Problems with Addition

Read the apartment ads and answer the questions.

a/c = air conditioning	din. rm. = dining room	nr. = near
BA = bathroom	kit. = kitchen	schl. = school
beaut. = beautiful	lge. = large	refrig. = refrigerator
BR = bedroom	liv. rm. = living room	

SPRINGFIELD 2 BR, new kit., lge. liv. rm., 1 BA. a/c. $1,250. Call (351) 378-2185.

RIVERDALE 3 BR, new refrig. in kit., din. rm., beaut. liv. rm., 2 BA, nr. schl. $1,825. Call (562) 471-0953.

1. How many rooms are there in the Springfield apartment?
   a. Three rooms plus one bathroom
   b. Four rooms plus one bathroom
   c. Four rooms plus two bathrooms
   d. Five rooms plus one bathroom

2. Marta is renting the Springfield apartment. She's writing a check for the first month's rent plus a one-month security deposit. She's paying _____.
   a. $1,500
   b. $1,750
   c. $2,500
   d. $2,600

3. How many rooms are there in the Riverdale apartment?
   a. Three rooms plus three bathrooms
   b. Four rooms plus two bathrooms
   c. Five rooms plus two bathrooms
   d. Six rooms plus two bathrooms

4. Nick is renting the Riverdale apartment. He's writing a check for the first month's rent plus a one-month security deposit. He's paying _____.
   a. $3,650
   b. $3,700
   c. $3,825
   d. $3,900

Write the correct answer in words.

5. Richard's apartment has many windows. There are two windows in the kitchen, two windows in the living room, three windows in the bedroom, and one window in the bathroom. How many windows are there in his apartment?

   _____

6. There are six apartments in Richard's building. Three people live in Apartment 1, four people live in Apartment 2, three people live in Apartment 3, six people live in Apartment 4, and two people live in Apartment 5. Richard lives in Apartment 6. How many neighbors does he have?

   _____

A CLOTHING TAGS

Look at the clothing tags and answer the questions.

```
Men's
100% Polyester
Color: Blue
Size: L
$29.00
```

1. What size is this?   _____

2. How much is it?   _____

3. What color is it?   _____

```
50% cotton
50% polyester
CLR: Pink
Size: S
$12.00
```

4. What size is this?   _____

5. How much is it?   _____

6. What color is it?   _____

B A CLOTHING STORE AD

Look at the ad and answer the questions.

GRANT'S DEPARTMENT STORE

End of Winter Sale

NOW **$39.99**
Reg. $65.00
Sizes:
S, M, L

NOW **$10.00**
Reg. $20.00
one size fits all

NOW **$9.50**
Reg. $19.95
Sizes: S, M, L

NOW **$59.99**
Reg. $125.00
Sizes:
S, M, L, XL

NOW **$59.50**
Reg. $125.00
Sizes: 6–10

1. What's the regular price of the men's jackets?   _____

2. What's the sale price of the men's jackets?   _____

3. What's the regular price of the gloves?   _____

4. What's the sale price of the gloves?   _____

5. What sizes are the women's winter boots?   _____

6. How much are the women's boots now?   _____

7. What sizes are the men's coats?   _____

8. How much are the men's coats now?   _____

C STORE RECEIPTS

Look at the receipts and answer the questions.

```
         Receipt
       Thank you for
  shopping at Clothing World
MEN'S JEANS        $40.00
MEN'S SUITS        $89.00
SUBTOTAL          $129.00
SALES TAX 5%        $6.45
TOTAL             $135.45
```

1. How much are the jeans? _____

2. How much is the suit? _____

3. How much is the tax? _____

4. How much is the person paying? _____

```
          Receipt
 Wilson's Department Store
CHILDREN'S PAJAMAS    $14.50
WOMEN'S HATS          $24.00
SUBTOTAL              $38.50
SALES TAX 4%           $1.54
TOTAL                $40.04
```

5. How much are the pajamas? _____

6. How much is the hat? _____

7. How much is the tax? _____

8. How much is the person paying? _____

D NUMERACY: Word Problems with Subtraction

Solve the word problems.

1. Carol is buying a blouse. It costs $18.50.
   She's paying with a twenty-dollar bill.
   What's her change?

   $20.00 − $18.50 = _____

   a. $1.50
   b. $2.50
   c. $.50

2. Roberto is buying a shirt. It costs $42.98.
   He's paying with a fifty-dollar bill. What's
   his change?
   a. $8.02
   b. $7.02
   c. $18.02

3. Marisol is buying a pair of shoes. They
   cost $34.89. She's paying with two twenty-
   dollar bills. What's her change?
   a. $6.11
   b. $5.21
   c. $5.11

4. Dennis is buying a suit. It costs $86.75.
   He's paying with a hundred dollar bill.
   What's his change?
   a. $13.25
   b. $14.25
   c. $12.35

E NUMERACY: Store Receipt Calculations

1. Add the prices of the shirt and the pants together and fill in
   the missing **subtotal.**
2. Add the sales tax to the subtotal and fill in the missing **total.**
3. Subtract the total from the cash payment ($100 − total) and
   fill in the **change.**

The shirt and pants plus tax cost $_____ [4]. The customer is

giving $_____ [5] and getting $_____ [6] change.

```
Fifth Avenue Sportswear
Shirt                35.99
Pants                52.98
Subtotal            _____ 1
Sales Tax             4.44
Total               _____ 2
Cash Payment       100.00
Change              _____ 3
```

A NUMERACY: Percentages and a Bar Graph

Read the information and study the bar graph. Match the percentages with the correct information.

Interviewers asked 3,204 Americans how they get the news on a typical day. This graph shows what percent get their news from television, the newspaper, the radio, and the Internet. The graph also shows what percent spend 30 minutes or more every day getting the news.

STUDENT BOOK
PAGES **86a–86b**

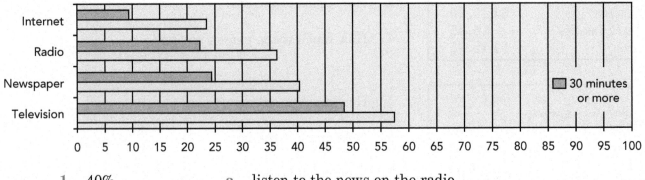

_____ 1. 40%

_____ 2. 57%

_____ 3. 36%

_____ 4. 24%

_____ 5. 9%

a. listen to the news on the radio

b. get news online on the Internet for 30 minutes or more

c. read the newspaper

d. watch the news on TV

e. read the newspaper for 30 minutes or more

B NUMERACY: A Line Graph

Study the line graph. Circle the number of minutes each age group spends getting the news.

This graph shows the average number of minutes different age groups spend getting the news on a typical day.

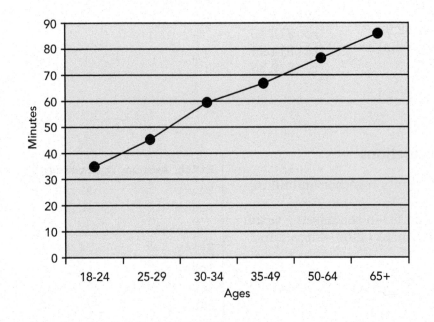

1. 30–34 years old   46   52   59

2. 18–24 years old   25   30   35

3. 50–64 years old   69   76   80

4. 25–29 years old   45   50   54

5. 35–49 years old   60   66   78

6. 65 years old +   80   85   90

A WORK SCHEDULES

Match the conversation with the correct work schedule.

_____ 1. A. When do you work this week?
   B. I work on Thursday, Friday, and Saturday.

S	M	T	W	T	F	S
✓	✓	✓			✓	✓

a.

_____ 2. A. When are your days off this week?
   B. I don't work on Wednesday and Thursday.

S	M	T	W	T	F	S
		✓	✓			

b.

_____ 3. A. When do you work this week?
   B. I work on Tuesday and Wednesday.

S	M	T	W	T	F	S
				✓	✓	✓

c.

STUDENT BOOK
PAGES **96a–96b**

B NUMERACY: Word Problems with Multiplication

Solve the word problems.

1. Rafael and three friends are going to a rock concert. Rafael is buying the tickets. Each ticket costs $15.00. How much money does Rafael need?
   a. Forty-five dollars
   b. Fifty dollars
   c. Sixty dollars
   d. Sixty-five dollars

2. Mr. and Mrs. Nardone are taking their son and daughter and their daughter's two friends to a baseball game. Tickets cost $18. How much are they spending?
   a. One hundred eight dollars
   b. One hundred eighteen dollars
   c. One hundred thirty-eight dollars
   d. One hundred forty-eight dollars

3. Ms. Martin's class is going to the Museum of Science. It costs $9 to get into the museum. Ms. Martin is buying sixteen tickets. How much is she spending?
   a. Ninety-five dollars
   b. One hundred forty-four dollars
   c. One hundred fifty-four dollars
   d. One hundred fifty-three dollars

4. Mr. and Mrs. Wang and their three children are going to the movies. Movie tickets cost $12 for adults and $6 for children. How much are they spending?
   a. Thirty-six dollars
   b. Forty-two dollars
   c. Forty-six dollars
   d. Forty-eight dollars

5. Alice gets eight days off every month. How many days off does she get in a year?
   a. Eighty
   b. Eighty-six
   c. Ninety-two
   d. Ninety-six

6. Harvey goes to school during the week and works at his father's store every Saturday and Sunday. How many days does he work in a year?
   a. One hundred two
   b. One hundred four
   c. One hundred twelve
   d. One hundred fourteen

7. Rosa works five days a week. She has a four-week vacation, so she works forty-eight weeks in a year. How many days does she work in a year?
   a. Two hundred forty
   b. Two hundred forty-five
   c. Two hundred fifty
   d. Two hundred sixty

8. Rodney works seventeen days every month at the Jefferson Hotel. How many days does he work in a year?
   a. One hundred seventy
   b. One hundred ninety-four
   c. Two hundred four
   d. Three hundred four

Activity Workbook   155

A DESCRIBING PEOPLE

What do they look like? Write a description of each person.

Tom

John

| tall |
| short |
| heavy |
| thin |
| curly |
| straight |
| gray |
| black |

1. Tom is _____, and he has _____.

2. John is _____, and he has _____.

B NUMERACY: Word Problems with Mixed Operations

Solve the word problems.

1. Diane is paying the bills. Her telephone bill is $46.55, her electric bill is $38.96, and her gas bill is $72.33. How much money does she need to pay all three bills?
   a. $147.85   c. $157.84
   b. $156.84   d. $167.84

2. Alfred spends $145 for gas and electricity every month. His gas bill is always $87. How much is his electric bill?
   a. $58   c. $132
   b. $68   d. $232

3. Luisa cleans rooms in a hotel. She works thirty-five hours a week and cleans four rooms in an hour. How many rooms does she clean in a week?
   a. 40   c. 135
   b. 130   d. 140

4. Orlando is buying groceries. They cost $118.76. He's paying with six twenty-dollar bills. What's his change?
   a. $.24   c. $2.24
   b. $1.24   d. $21.24

5. Marilyn spends $60 a week on groceries. How much does she spend in a year?
   a. $720   c. $3,020
   b. $1,110   d. $3,120

6. Bernard buys groceries twice a month. He usually spends $100 when he's at the store. How much does he spend in a year?
   a. $1,200   c. $2,400
   b. $2,200   d. $5,200

7. When Jay does his laundry at the laundromat, he puts eight quarters in the washing machine and four quarters in the clothes dryer. How much does he spend when he does his laundry?
   a. $2.50   c. $4.00
   b. $3.00   d. $5.00

8. Jay does his laundry at the laundromat once a week. Based on the information in question 7, how much does he spend in a year?
   a. $12.00   c. $52.00
   b. $24.00   d. $156.00

156   Activity Workbook

A PEOPLE AND PLACES AT SCHOOL

Match the school personnel with their actions.

_____ 1. The principal   a. manages the library.

_____ 2. The librarian   b. cleans the school.

_____ 3. The school nurse   c. take the students home.

_____ 4. The cafeteria workers   d. manages the school.

_____ 5. The custodian   e. serve lunch to the students.

_____ 6. The school secretary   f. takes care of the students when they are sick.

_____ 7. The bus drivers   g. answers the telephone.

STUDENT BOOK
PAGES **114a–114b**

B NUMERACY: Percentages and a Pie Graph

There are 10,000 students in the Rosedale schools. 10% of the students (1,000 students) are at King Elementary School, and 8% of the students (800 students) are at Lincoln Elementary School. Look at the graph. Decide if the sentences are True (T) or False (F).

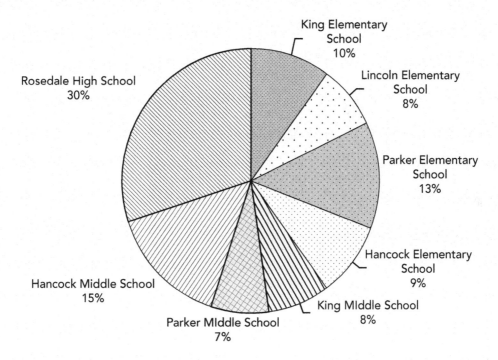

_____ 1. 13% of the students in the Rosedale schools go to Parker Elementary School.

_____ 2. 9% of the students go to King Middle School.

_____ 3. 30% of the students are in high school.

_____ 4. 28% of the students go to a middle school.

_____ 5. 40% of the students go to an elementary school.

_____ 6. There are 700 students at Parker Middle School.

_____ 7. Rosedale High School has 300 students.

_____ 8. More than 50% of the students in the Rosedale schools are in high school or middle school.

Activity Workbook   **157**

A JOB INTERESTS AND WORK SKILLS

What kind of jobs are these people looking for? Write the correct occupations.

building superintendent	mechanic	security guard
cashier	salesperson	waiter
chef		

1. I can fix cars. _____*mechanic*_____

2. I can talk to customers and take inventory. _____

3. I can use a cash register and handle money. _____

4. I can cook and bake. _____

5. I can paint walls and repair things. _____

6. I can inspect bags and packages. _____

7. I can take orders and serve food. _____

B HELP WANTED AD ABBREVIATIONS

Write the full words next to the abbreviations.

evenings	experience	part-time
excellent	full-time	required

1. PT _____   3. eves. _____   5. req. _____

2. FT _____   4. exper. _____   6. excel. _____

C READING HELP WANTED ADS

FT TRUCK DRIVER Position
License req. Excel salary.
Call Mr. Rupo at (207) 524-2255.

PT Security Guard Needed
Eves. M-F. $9/hr. No exp. req.
Apply in person. Multiplex Cinema.
3100 Lake Parkway.

1. The truck driver has to _____.
   a. have experience
   b. apply in person
   c. have a license
   d. work part-time

2. The ad for a truck driver has _____.
   a. the work days
   b. the name of the person to call
   c. the experience required
   d. the name of the business

3. The security guard has to _____.
   a. call for an application
   b. have experience
   c. work full-time
   d. apply in person

4. The ad for the security guard doesn't have _____.
   a. the salary
   b. the name of the business
   c. the number of work hours
   d. the work days

D JOB APPLICATION FORM

Complete the job application. You can use real or made-up information.

Sandwich Express Employment Application

Last Name: _____ First Name: _____

Address: _____

Phone: Day _____ Evening _____ Cell _____

What job are you applying for? _____

Availability—Circle one: **Circle all the days you are available to work.**

Full-Time   Part-Time   S   M   T   W   T   F   S

What time of day are you available? Circle one: mornings   afternoons   evenings

Work Skills: (Tell about your skills and abilities.)

_____

_____

E NUMERACY: Word Problems with Division

Solve the word problems.

1. Larry makes $12.00 an hour and usually makes $480 a week. How many hours does he usually work in a week?
   a. 20 hours
   b. 30 hours
   c. 40 hours
   d. 45 hours

2. Karen works twenty hours a week. Her salary is $300 a week. How much does she make an hour?
   a. $10
   b. $15
   c. $18
   d. $24

3. Laura works eight hours a day and makes $108.00 each day. How much does she make an hour?
   a. $8.00
   b. $10.80
   c. $13.40
   d. $13.50

4. Don needs $3,600 to buy a computer. He makes $600 a week. How many weeks does he have to work to make $3,600?
   a. Five weeks
   b. Six weeks
   c. Seven weeks
   d. Eight weeks

5. Alex makes $12 an hour. His weekly salary is $420. How many hours a week does he work?
   a. 35 hours
   b. 36 hours
   c. 38 hours
   d. 40 hours

6. Gina makes $30,000 a year. How much does she make a month?
   a. $250
   b. $2,500
   c. $2,800
   d. $3,000

7. Janet usually works thirty hours and makes $330 a week. This week she is working fifteen hours. How much is her salary this week?
   a. $150
   b. $160
   c. $165
   d. $315

8. Sam works 30 hours a week and makes $10 an hour. Last week he made $375 because he worked 5 hours overtime. How much does he make per overtime hour?
   a. $5.00
   b. $10.00
   c. $15.00
   d. $20.00

A NUMERACY: Ordinal Numbers

Write the correct ordinal number.

1. eighth _____
2. fifteenth _____
3. first _____
4. ninetieth _____

5. second _____
6. sixtieth _____
7. tenth _____
8. third _____

9. thirteenth _____
10. thirty-first _____
11. twenty-fourth _____
12. twenty-second _____

B MONTHS AND ORDINAL NUMBERS

Which month of the year is it? Write the answers two ways.

1. June _____sixth_____ ___6th___
2. April _____ _____
3. July _____ _____

4. December _____ _____
5. November _____ _____
6. March _____ _____

C NUMERACY: Writing Dates

Write these dates two ways.

1. July fifth, two thousand eighteen _____July 5, 2018_____ __7__/_15_/_18_
2. April nineteenth, nineteen seventy-six _____ ___/___/___
3. March twenty-second, two thousand fifteen _____ ___/___/___
4. January thirty-first, nineteen ninety-four _____ ___/___/___
5. August twentieth, two thousand twenty _____ ___/___/___
6. Your date of birth _____ ___/___/___
7. Today's date _____ ___/___/___

D AN EMPLOYMENT AVAILABILITY SCHEDULE

Look at the employment application. Decide if the sentences are T (True) or F (False).

> **Personal Information:**
> Name: _Lucy Chang_
>
> **Availability:**
> Check one: Part-time _X_ Full-time _____
>
> Please list all the times you are available to work (from 6 A.M. to 12 A.M.):
> M _8-1_   T _8-1_   W _8-12_   TH _8-1_   F _8-2:30_   SAT _1-5:30_   SUN _1-5:30_

_____ 1. Lucy can work part-time.

_____ 2. Lucy can begin work at eight o'clock every morning.

_____ 3. Lucy can work five and a half hours on Saturday.

_____ 4. Lucy can work on Sunday afternoons.

_____ 5. Lucy can work until half past five on Tuesday.

_____ 6. Lucy can't work at 1:00 on Wednesday.

E A BANK SCHEDULE

Look at the sign and answer the questions.

Central Bank		HOURS OF OPERATION	
MONDAY	9:00 – 5:00	FRIDAY	9:00 – 7:00
TUESDAY	9:00 – 5:00	SATURDAY	9:00 – 11:30
WEDNESDAY	9:00 – 3:00	SUNDAY	CLOSED
THURSDAY	9:00 – 7:00		

1. The bank is open ____.
   a. all day on Saturday
   b. on Sunday
   c. all day Friday
   d. on Wednesday evening

2. The bank closes at seven o'clock on ____.
   a. Friday and Saturday
   b. Thursday
   c. Monday and Tuesday
   d. Thursday and Friday

3. The bank is open for two and half hours on ____.
   a. Saturday
   b. Sunday
   c. Friday
   d. Monday

4. The bank is closed on ____.
   a. Wednesday afternoon
   b. Sunday
   c. Friday morning
   d. Thursday evening

F NUMERACY: Elapsed Time

Look at the bus schedule. Decide if the sentences are True (T) or False (F).

Harrison Ave.	Elm St.	Columbia St.	Lee St.	Wilson Ave.	Market St.
7:15 A.M.	7:32 A.M.	7:55 A.M.	8:15 A.M.	8:50 A.M.	9:20 A.M.
9:45 A.M.	10:00 A.M.	10:21 A.M.	10:39 A.M.	11:12 A.M.	11:40 A.M.
12:30 P.M.	————	1:02 P.M.	1:20 P.M.	1:53 P.M.	2:21 P.M.
3:15 P.M.	————	3:47 P.M.	4:05 P.M.	4:38 P.M.	5:06 P.M.
5:45 P.M.	6:02 P.M.	6:25 P.M.	6:45 P.M.	7:20 P.M.	7:50 P.M.

_____ 1. It takes 30 minutes to go from Wilson Ave. to Market St. at 8:50 A.M.

_____ 2. It takes 21 minutes to go from Elm St. to Columbia St. at 7:32 A.M.

_____ 3. It takes 20 minutes to go from Columbia St. to Lee St. at 6:25 P.M.

_____ 4. It takes 20 minutes to go from Columbia St. to Lee St. at 3:47 P.M.

_____ 5. It takes 30 minutes to go from Harrison Ave. to Columbia St. at 5:45 P.M.

_____ 6. It takes 50 minutes to go from Harrison Ave. to Lee St. at 12:30 P.M.

_____ 7. It takes an hour and 22 minutes to go from Elm St. to Wilson Ave. at 6:02 P.M.

_____ 8. It takes 2 hours and 5 minutes to go from Harrison Ave. to Market St. at 7:15 A.M.

_____ 9. It always takes 2 hours and 5 minutes to go from Harrison Ave. to Market St.

A A MEDICAL EXAM

Complete the sentences with the correct words.

check	listen	open	sit	take
get	measure	say	stand	

1. _____ on the scale.

2. _____ on the examination table.

3. _____ a deep breath.

4. _____ your mouth.

5. _____ "Ahh!"

6. _____ dressed.

7. I'm going to _____ your height.

8. I'm going to _____ to your heart.

9. I'm going to _____ your reflexes.

B MEDICAL APPOINTMENT CARDS

Look at the appointment cards. Decide if the sentences are True (T) or False (F).

Janet Reid, M.D.

Jim Gluck

has an appointment

DATE: ___9/30___ TIME: _3:45 P.M._

MON. __ TUE. __ WED. __THURS. __ FRI. X

DR. DONALD MILLER

Pam Wong

My appointment is on

M   T   W   (T)   F

DATE: _7/10_   TIME: _4:20 P.M._

Dr. Adam Ko

Amy White

has an appointment on

Mon	Feb	2
day	month	date

At _11:30_   ✓ A.M. _____ P.M.

DR. MARIA FERNANDEZ

Your next appointment

Brenda Franklin

Day	Date	Hour
Tues	_10/7_	_10:15 A.M._

_____ 1. Jim Gluck has an appointment with Dr. Miller.

_____ 2. Jim has an appointment in the morning.

_____ 3. Jim has an appointment in September.

_____ 4. Amy White has an appointment on 2/2.

_____ 5. Amy has an appointment at half past twelve.

_____ 6. Amy has an appointment with Dr. Ko.

_____ 7. Pam Wong has an appointment with Dr. Reid.

_____ 8. Pam has an appointment on October 10.

(continued)

_____ 9. Pam has an appointment in the afternoon.

_____ 10. Brenda has an appointment on Thursday.

_____ 11. Brenda's appointment is in the morning.

_____ 12. Brenda's appointment is on July 10.

C NUMERACY: Math & Dosage Instructions on Medicine Labels

Look at the medicine labels. Decide if the sentences are True (T) or False (F).

Benson's Aspirin

Dosage:

Adults and children 12 years and over:	Take 4 to 6 pills twice a day with water.
Children under 12: Use before 8/4/21.	Consult a doctor.

Marvel Cough Syrup

adults & children 12 years and over	2 teaspoons 3 times a day
children 6 years to under 12 years	1 teaspoon 3 times a day
children 2 years to under 6 years	1/2 teaspoon 3 times a day
children under 2 years	Ask a doctor.

Do not use for more than 7 days.

Rubetam Cold Medicine

Age	Dosage
adults & children 12 years and over	2 tablets every 4 hours
children 6 years to under 12 years	1 tablet every 4 hours
children 2 years to under 6 years	1/2 tablet every 4 hours
children under 2 years	Ask a doctor.

Do not take more than 4 doses in any 24-hour period.

Walton's Pain Reliever

Directions:

Adults and children 12 years and over:	Take 2 capsules every 4 to 6 hours with food.
Children under 12:	Do not use this product unless directed by a doctor.

Use before 4/8/21.

_____ 1. Adults can take six teaspoons of Marvel Cough Syrup a day.

_____ 2. Adults can take 16 Benson's Aspirin pills in a day.

_____ 3. Eight-year-old children can take 21 teaspoons of Marvel Cough Syrup in a week.

_____ 4. Adults can take four Rubetam Cold Medicine tablets in seven hours.

_____ 5. Adults can take Walton's Pain Reliever four to six times in 24 hours.

_____ 6. Adults can take 24 Walton's Pain Reliever tablets in two days.

_____ 7. Five-year old children can take two teaspoons of Marvel Cough Syrup a day.

_____ 8. You can take Walton's Pain Reliever on July 3, 2021.

_____ 9. Adults can take more than 80 Benson's Aspirin pills in a week.

_____ 10. Adults _can't_ take more than 42 teaspoons of Marvel Cough Syrup in a week.

_____ 11. Adults can take ten tablets of Rubetam Cold Medicine in a day.

_____ 12. Two-year-old children _can't_ take more than 2 tablets of Rubetam Cold Medicine in a day.

Read the job application. Match the questions and answers.

16
STUDENT BOOK
PAGES 156a–156d

JOB APPLICATION FORM

Personal Information

Last Name: __Herrera__   First Name: __Rosa__

EDUCATION

School Name	Location	Dates Attended
High School: __Lincoln High School__	__Denver__	__9/10-6/14__
College: _____	_____	_____
Other: __LV Technical Institute__	__Las Vegas__	__9/14-6/15__

EMPLOYMENT RECORD (List most recent first)

Name of Employer: __Weston Offices__

Address: __310 Washington Ave., Las Vegas NV 89106__   Phone: __(702) 651-2231__

Dates: from __6/15__ to __present__   Position: __receptionist__

Salary: __$450/wk__   Reason for Leaving: __want more responsibility__

Name of Employer: __Graphic Line, Inc.__

Address: __100 Perry Ave., Denver, CO 80219__   Phone: __(702) 298-7575__

Dates: from __1/13__ to __7/14__   Position: __part-time office assistant__

Salary: __$7/hr__   Reason for Leaving: __moved to Las Vegas__

_____ 1. Where did Rosa go to high school?

_____ 2. When did Rosa go to high school?

_____ 3. Where did Rosa go after high school?

_____ 4. Where is Rosa working now?

_____ 5. What's her job now?

_____ 6. How long did she work as an office assistant?

_____ 7. Why did she leave the office assistant job?

_____ 8. Why does she want to leave her job now?

a. For a year and a half.

b. Because she moved.

c. She's a receptionist.

d. Lincoln High School in Denver.

e. Weston Offices.

f. Because she wants more responsibility.

g. From September 2010 to June 2014.

h. LV Technical Institute.

B FILLING OUT A JOB APPLICATION FORM

Complete the job application. You can use real or made-up information.

PERSONAL INFORMATION

Last Name: _____ First Name: _____

Home Address: _____

City: _____ State: _____ Zip Code: _____

Social Security Number: _____

Phone: Home _____ Cell _____

What job are you applying for?_____

AVAILABILITY

Circle one: Full-time   Part-time

What days are you available?   SUN   MON   TUE   WED   THU   FRI   SAT

What times of day are you available?   mornings   afternoons   evenings

EDUCATION

	School Name	Location	Dates Attended
High School:	_____	_____	_____
College:	_____	_____	_____
Other:	_____	_____	_____

EMPLOYMENT RECORD (List most recent first.)

Name of Employer: _____ Supervisor: _____

Address: _____ Phone: _____

Dates: from _____ to _____ Position: _____

Salary: _____ Reason for Leaving: _____

Name of Employer: _____ Supervisor: _____

Address: _____ Phone: _____

Dates: from _____ to _____ Position: _____

Salary: _____ Reason for Leaving: _____

WORK SKILLS: (List any special skills and abilities.)

_____

_____

NUMERACY: Elapsed Time & Amounts of Money

Look at Gina Moreno's job application. Decide if the sentences are True (T) or False (F).

EDUCATION

Name of School	Location	Dates Attended
High School: Miami Central Senior High School	Miami, FL	8/86–5/90
College: Miami Dade College	Miami, FL	8/91–5/93
Florida International University	Miami, FL	8/97–5/99
Other: Florida Cooking Academy	Orlando, FL	8/02–5/04

EMPLOYMENT RECORD (LIST MOST RECENT EMPLOYMENT FIRST)

Date From – To	Name & Address of Employer	Position	Salary	Name of Supervisor
9/1/11–9/15/16	Regent Hotel 1486 Terrace Rd., Jacksonville, FL	cook	$36,000/yr.	Hector Martinez
8/15/04–8/15/11	Ocean Seafood Restaurant 672 Harbor Drive, Orlando, FL	cook	$2,300/mo.	Cindy Larson
6/1/00–9/1/02	Kingman's Department Store 754 Grant Street, Miami, FL	salesperson	$7.50/hr.	Margaret Drew
11/1/94–9/1/97	Wellington Associates 4522 Ocean Blvd., Miami, FL	receptionist	$250/wk.	Mark Hubbard
8/15/93–12/15/94	Metropolitan Restaurant 350 Central Ave., Miami, FL	waitress	$5.25/hr.	Win Lee

_____ 1. Gina went to college for four years.

_____ 2. Gina went to cooking school for 2½ years.

_____ 3. Gina worked as a cook for twelve years.

_____ 4. Gina made $3,000 a month at the Regent Hotel.

_____ 5. When Gina worked as a waitress, she made $225 in a forty-hour week.

_____ 6. She made more than $6 an hour as a receptionist in a forty-hour week.

_____ 7. Gina worked at Wellington Associates for two years and eleven months.

_____ 8. Gina worked at Kingman's Department Store for twenty-seven months.

_____ 9. When she worked at Kingman's, she made more than $300 in a forty-hour week.

_____ 10. Gina made $27,600 a year at Ocean Seafood Restaurant.

_____ 11. Gina didn't work for a year after she graduated from Miami Dade College.

_____ 12. She didn't work for a year after she graduated from Florida International University.

A A SUPERMARKET AD

Look at the advertisement. Decide if the sentences are correct. Circle T for True and F for False.

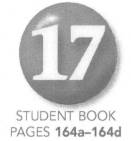

1. A quart of milk costs $2.00.	T	F
2. Five cans of black beans cost $4.00.	T	F
3. Three pounds of carrots cost $3.00.	T	F
4. Two pounds of Annie's American Cheese cost $8.00.	T	F
5. The price of Polly's Ice Cream is $3.50 a gallon.	T	F
6. Six cans of Charlie's Chicken Soup cost $12.	T	F

B FOOD LABELS

Look at the food labels and answer the questions.

1. What's the first ingredient in both cans? _____

2. What ingredients do both cans have? _____

3. Which can has sugar? _____

4. Which can has onions? _____

Activity Workbook **167**

Look at the supermarket ad and answer the questions.

$HOP & $AVE SUPERMARKET

Sunrise Orange Juice $2.15 Quart

Healthy Flakes Cereal 3 for $4.50

Tomatoes 3 pounds for $2.94

Tracy's Ice Cream $3.25 One Pint *Buy one. Get one free.*

Bananas 48¢ Per Pound

Shop & Save Vegetable Soup 4/$5

1. How much is a pound of tomatoes?   a. $.78   b. $.88   c. $.98

2. How much are two pounds of bananas?   a. $.48   b. $.96   c. $2.00

3. How much are six boxes of cereal?   a. $6.00   b. $9.00   c. $27.00

4. How much is a can of vegetable soup?   a. $1.25   b. $1.30   c. $1.50

5. How much are two boxes of cereal?   a. $1.50   b. $2.50   c. $3.00

6. How much are six pounds of tomatoes?   a. $5.88   b. $6.00   c. $17.64

7. How many cans of soup can you buy for $25?   a. 15   b. 20   c. 25

8. There are four quarts in a gallon.
   How much is a gallon of orange juice?   a. $8.60   b. $8.70   c. $8.80

9. There are two pints in a quart.
   How much is a quart of Tracy's Ice Cream? a. $1.63   b. $3.25   c. $6.50

10. There are sixteen ounces in a pound.
    How much are 1 pound, 8 ounces of tomatoes?   a. $1.47   b. $1.58   c. $1.69

Listening Scripts

Page 3 Exercise C

Listen and circle the number you hear.

1. My address is five Main Street.
2. My address is seven Main Street.
3. My address is two Main Street.
4. My address is six Main Street.
5. My address is one Main Street.
6. My address is three Main Street.
7. My address is four Main Street.
8. My address is eight Main Street.
9. My address is ten Main Street.
10. My address is nine Main Street.

Page 4 Exercise E

Listen and write the missing numbers.

1. A. What's your phone number?
   B. My phone number is 389-7932.
2. A. What's your telephone number?
   B. My telephone number is 837-2953.
3. A. What's your apartment number?
   B. My apartment number is 6-B.
4. A. What's your address?
   B. My address is 10 Main Street.
5. A. What's your fax number?
   B. My fax number is 654-7315.
6. A. What's your license number?
   B. My license number is 2613498.

Page 5 Exercise F

Listen and write the missing letters.

1. A. What's your last name?
   B. Carter.
   A. How do you spell that?
   B. C-A-R-T-E-R.
2. A. What's your last name?
   B. Johnson.
   A. How do you spell that?
   B. J-O-H-N-S-O-N.
3. A. What's your first name?
   B. Gerald.
   A. How do you spell that?
   B. G-E-R-A-L-D.
4. A. What's your last name?
   B. Anderson.
   A. How do you spell that?
   B. A-N-D-E-R-S-O-N.
5. A. What's your first name?
   B. Phillip.
   A. How do you spell that?
   B. P-H-I-L-L-I-P.
6. A. What's your last name?
   B. Martinez.
   A. How do you spell that?
   B. M-A-R-T-I-N-E-Z.

Page 6 Exercise B

Listen and put a check under the correct picture.

1. A. Where's the book?
   B. It's on the desk.
2. A. Where's the dictionary?
   B. It's on the chair.
3. A. Where's the ruler?
   B. It's on the desk.
4. A. Where's the map?
   B. It's on the bulletin board.
5. A. Where's the globe?
   B. It's on the bookshelf.

6. A. Where's the computer?
   B. It's on the table.

Page 11 Exercise J

Listen and write the number under the correct picture.

1. Our English teacher is in the hospital.
2. Mr. and Mrs. Sanchez are in the restaurant.
3. Mary is at the dentist.
4. Billy and Jimmy are in the park.
5. Mr. and Mrs. Lee are at the social security office.
6. James is home in bed.

Page 11 Exercise K

Listen and circle the word you hear.

1. Where are you?
2. Ms. Jones is in the bank.
3. We're friends.
4. Hi. How are you?
5. Where's the newspaper?
6. He's from Korea.
7. The computer is on the table.
8. It's in the bathroom.

Page 15 Exercise C

Listen and put a check under the correct picture.

1. He's eating lunch.
2. We're drinking milk.
3. I'm playing the guitar.
4. She's playing the piano.
5. We're cooking breakfast.
6. It's in the classroom.
7. I'm reading.
8. He's watching TV.
9. She's studying mathematics.
10. They're playing baseball in the yard.

Page 20 Exercise D

Listen and write the letter or number you hear.

Ex. A. What's your first name?
   B. Mark.
   A. How do you spell that?
   B. M-A-R-K.
1. A. What's your last name?
   B. Carter.
   A. How do you spell that?
   B. C-A-R-T-E-R.
2. A. What's your telephone number?
   B. My telephone number is 354-9812.
3. A. What's your fax number?
   B. My fax number is 890-7462.
4. A. What's your first name?
   B. Julie.
   A. How do you spell that?
   B. J-U-L-I-E.
5. A. What's your telephone number?
   B. My telephone number is 672-3059.
6. A. What's your license number?
   B. My license number is 5170349.

Page 22 Exercise C

Listen and circle the word you hear.

1. We're cleaning our room.
2. He's doing his homework.
3. She's washing her hair.
4. They're fixing their car.
5. You're fixing your TV.
6. I'm feeding my cat.

Page 24 Exercise G

Listen and circle the word you hear.

1. He's studying.
2. She's doing her homework.
3. I'm feeding my cat.

(continued)

4. He's cleaning his yard.
5. We're fixing our car.
6. They're washing their clothes.

Page 27 Exercise C

Listen and circle the word you hear.

1. Sally's brother is very tall.
2. Their dog is very heavy.
3. The questions in my English book are very easy.
4. My friend George is single.
5. Mary's cat is very ugly!
6. This book is very cheap.

Page 32 Exercise K

Listen and circle the word you hear.

1. A. How's the weather in Rome today?
   B. It's cool.
2. A. How's the weather in Tokyo today?
   B. It's snowing.
3. A. How's the weather in Seoul today?
   B. It's sunny.
4. A. How's the weather in Shanghai today?
   B. It's hot.
5. A. How's the weather in New York today?
   B. It's raining.
6. A. How's the weather in Miami today?
   B. It's cloudy.

Page 34 Exercise O

Listen to the temperature in Fahrenheit and Celsius. Write the numbers you hear.

1. In Los Angeles, it's 86° Fahrenheit/30° Celsius.
2. In Seoul, it's 32° Fahrenheit/0° Celsius.
3. In San Juan, it's 81° Fahrenheit/27° Celsius.
4. In Hong Kong, it's 72° Fahrenheit/22° Celsius.
5. In Miami, it's 93° Fahrenheit/34° Celsius.
6. In London, it's 56° Fahrenheit/13° Celsius.
7. In Mexico City, it's 66° Fahrenheit/19° Celsius.
8. In Moscow, it's 34° Fahrenheit/1° Celsius.

Page 36 Exercise B

Listen and put a check under the correct picture.

1. In this photograph, my sister is skateboarding in the park.
2. In this photograph, my son is acting in a play.
3. In this photograph, my friends are dancing at my wedding.
4. In this photograph, my uncle is baking a cake.
5. In this photograph, my cousin is playing a game on her computer.
6. In this photograph, my husband is standing in front of our apartment building.
7. In this photograph, my grandparents are having dinner.
8. In this photograph, my aunt is planting flowers.

Page 40 Exercise E

Listen and choose the correct response.

Ex. Is he old?

1. Is it large?
2. Is she poor?
3. Is it sunny?
4. Is he quiet?

Page 43 Exercise C

Listen to the sentences about the buildings on the map. After each sentence, write the name on the correct building.

1. There's a bakery between the barber shop and the bank.
2. There's a school next to the church.
3. There's a department store across from the school and the church.
4. There's a library around the corner from the barber shop.
5. There's a hospital across from the library.
6. There's a police station next to the hospital.
7. There's a hair salon across from the barber shop.
8. There's a supermarket next to the hair salon.
9. There's a video store around the corner from the bank.

10. There's a park between the library and the video store.
11. There's a health club around the corner from the department store.
12. There's a train station across from the health club.

Page 51 Exercise D

Listen and circle the word you hear.

1. umbrellas
2. blouses
3. coats
4. computer
5. shoes
6. exercises
7. dress
8. restaurants
9. necklaces
10. earring
11. belt
12. watches
13. nieces
14. nephew
15. shirts
16. tie

Page 52 Exercise E

Listen and circle the color you hear.

1. My favorite color is blue.
2. My favorite color is green.
3. My favorite color is gray.
4. My favorite color is silver.
5. My favorite color is yellow.
6. My favorite color is orange.

Page 54 Exercise H

Listen and put a check under the correct picture.

1. I'm washing these socks.
2. He's reading this book.
3. I'm looking for these men.
4. They're using these computers.
5. We're vacuuming this rug.
6. She's playing with these dogs.
7. We're painting this garage.
8. They're listening to these radios.

Page 54 Exercise I

Listen and circle the correct word to complete the sentence.

1. This bicycle . . .
2. These exercises . . .
3. These apartment buildings . . .
4. This bracelet . . .
5. These women . . .
6. These sunglasses . . .
7. This car . . .
8. These jeans . . .
9. This refrigerator . . .

Page 61 Exercise F

Listen and circle the correct word to complete the sentence.

Ex. These dresses . . .

1. That house . . .
2. Those people . . .
3. These flowers . . .
4. This blouse . . .

Page 63 Exercise B

Listen and choose the correct response.

1. What's your name?
2. What language do you speak?
3. What do they do every day?
4. Where do you live?
5. What language do you speak?
6. What do you do every day?

Page 66 Exercise G

Listen and circle the word you hear.

1. We live in Paris.
2. Where do you live?
3. What language does he speak?
4. Every day I listen to Greek music.
5. Every day she watches English TV shows.
6. What do they eat every day?
7. Every day I sing Korean songs.
8. Every day she eats Chinese food.
9. Every day he reads Mexican newspapers.

Page 70 Exercise D

Listen and choose the correct response.

1. What kind of food do you like?
2. Do they paint houses?
3. Why does he go to that restaurant?
4. When does Mrs. Miller cook dinner?
5. Do you work in a bank?
6. Where do they live?
7. What do your children do in the park?
8. Does your friend Patty drive a taxi?
9. Why do they shop in that store?

Page 72 Exercise I

Listen and choose the correct response.

1. Do you do a different kind of sport every day?
2. Does Bob write for the school newspaper?
3. Do Mr. and Mrs. Chang live near a bus stop?
4. Does your sister baby-sit every weekend?
5. Does Timmy do a different activity every day?
6. Do your children play in the orchestra?
7. Does your son sing in the choir?
8. Do your parents go to the park every day?
9. Do you play cards with your friends?

Page 75 Exercise D

Listen and choose the correct response.

Ex. What do Patty and Peter do during the week?

1. When do you watch your favorite TV program?
2. Why do you eat Italian food?
3. Does Carlos visit his grandparents in Puerto Rico?
4. What kind of books do you like?
5. Where do your nephews live?

Page 77 Exercise C

Listen and put a check under the correct picture.

1. How often do you read them?
2. I call her every day.
3. I don't like him.
4. I wash it every weekend.
5. He calls us all the time.
6. I say "hello" to them every morning.

Page 78 Exercise G

Listen and choose the correct answer.

1. Henry's car is always very dirty.
2. My husband sometimes makes dinner.
3. My neighbors play loud music at night.
4. My grandparents rarely speak English.
5. Jane always spends a lot of time with her friends.
6. I rarely study in the library.

Page 82 Exercise N

Listen and choose the correct response.

1. Do you have curly hair?
2. Are you married?
3. Does he have brown eyes?
4. Do you have a brother?
5. Do you usually go out on weekends?
6. Is your husband heavy?
7. Do you live in the city?
8. Do you have short hair?

Page 89 Exercise H

As you listen to each story, read the sentences and check yes **or** no.

Jennifer and Jason

Jennifer and Jason are visiting their grandfather in California. They're sad today. Their grandfather usually takes them to the park, but he isn't taking them to the park today.

Our Boss

Our boss usually smiles at the office, but he isn't smiling today. He's upset because the people in our office aren't working very

hard today. It's Friday, and everybody is thinking about the weekend.

On Vacation

When my family and I are on vacation, I always have a good time. I usually play tennis, but when it's cold, I play games on my computer and watch videos. Today is a beautiful day, and I'm swimming at the beach.

Timmy and His Brother

Timmy and his brother are watching a science fiction movie. Timmy is covering his eyes because he's scared. He doesn't like science fiction movies. Timmy's brother isn't scared. He likes science fiction movies.

Page 91 Exercise E

Listen and choose the correct response.

Ex. What are Peter and Tom doing today?

1. What do mail carriers do every day?
2. Where are you going today?
3. What do you do when you're scared?
4. Do you usually use a typewriter?
5. Where do you usually study?

Page 93 Exercise D

Listen and circle the word you hear.

1. Our teacher can speak French.
2. I can't play the piano.
3. He can paint houses.
4. My sister can play soccer.
5. They can't sing.
6. Can you drive a bus?
7. I can't read Japanese newspapers.
8. My son Tommy can play the drums.
9. Their children can't swim.
10. Can your husband cook?
11. We can't skate.
12. I can use a cash register.

Page 97 Exercise K

Listen and circle the words you hear.

1. We have to go to the supermarket.
2. My son has to play his violin every day.
3. We can use business software on our computers.
4. Boris has to speak English every day now.
5. I can't cook Italian food.
6. Apartment building superintendents have to repair locks and paint apartments.
7. That actress can't act!
8. Our children have to use a computer to do their homework.
9. Mr. Johnson can operate equipment.

Page 98 Exercise M

Listen and choose the correct answer.

1. I'm sorry. I can't go to the movies with you today. I have to go to the dentist.
2. I can't go to the party on Saturday. I have to wash my clothes.
3. I can't have lunch with you, but I can have dinner.
4. We can't go skiing this weekend. We have to paint our kitchen.
5. I'm very busy today. I have to go shopping, and I have to cook dinner for my family.
6. I can't see a play with you on Friday because I have to baby-sit. But I can see a play with you on Saturday.

Page 102 Exercise H

Listen and circle the words you hear.

1. I'm going to visit her this year.
2. I'm going to write to my uncle right away.
3. I'm going to call them this Monday.
4. When are you going to cut your hair?
5. I'm going to fix it next Tuesday.
6. We're going to see them this December.

(continued)

7. They're going to visit us this winter.
8. I'm going to clean it at once.
9. We're going to spend time with them this August.
10. I'm going to wash them immediately.
11. You're going to see us next week.
12. When are you going to call the plumber?

Page 103 Exercise J

Listen to the following weather forecasts and circle the correct answers.

Today's Weather Forecast

This is Mike Martinez with today's weather forecast. This afternoon it's going to be cool and cloudy, with temperatures from 50 to 55 degrees Fahrenheit. This evening it's going to be foggy and warm, but it isn't going to rain.

This Weekend's Weather Forecast

This is Barbara Burrows with your weekend weather forecast. Tonight it's going to be clear and warm, with 60 degree temperatures. On Saturday you can swim at the beach. It's going to be sunny and very hot, with temperatures between 90 and 95 degrees Fahrenheit. But take your umbrella with you on Sunday because it's going to be cool and it's going to rain.

Monday's Weather Forecast

This is Al Alberts with Monday's weather forecast. Monday morning it's going to be cool and nice, but Monday afternoon wear your gloves and your boots because it's going to be very cold and it's going to snow! On Tuesday morning the skiing is going to be wonderful because it's going to be sunny and very warm!

Page 108 Exercise T

Listen and write the time you hear.

1. It's seven forty-five.
2. It's six fifteen.
3. It's four thirty.
4. It's nine fifteen.
5. It's midnight.
6. It's five o'clock.
7. It's a quarter to nine.
8. It's a quarter after eight.
9. It's one forty-five.
10. It's noon.
11. It's eleven thirty.
12. It's a quarter to three.

Page 113 Exercise G

Listen to the story. Fill in the correct times.

Every day at school I study English, science, mathematics, music, and Chinese. English class begins at 8:30. I go to science at 10:15 and mathematics at 11:00. We have lunch at 12:15. We go to music at 12:45, and we have Chinese at 1:30.

Page 114 Exercise B

Listen to the story. Put the number under the correct picture.

Everybody in my family is sick today.

My parents are sick.
1. My father has a stomachache.
2. My mother has a backache.

My brother and my sister are sick, too.
3. My sister Alice has an earache.
4. My brother David has a toothache.

My grandparents are also sick.
5. My grandmother has a cold.
6. My grandfather has a sore throat.
7. Even my dog is sick! He has a fever!

Yes, everybody in my family is sick today . . . everybody except me!

How do I feel today?
8. I feel fine!

Page 117 Exercise F

Listen and circle the correct answer.

Example 1: I study.
Example 2: I played cards.

1. I planted flowers.
2. I shave.
3. I cried.
4. I typed.

5. I work.
6. I shouted.
7. I clean.
8. I studied.
9. I fixed my car.
10. I paint.
11. I smile.
12. I cooked.

Page 126 Exercise I

Listen and choose the correct response.

1. When did you write to your girlfriend?
2. When does your neighbor wash his car?
3. Who did your parents visit?
4. Where does Irene do yoga?
5. When did your son go to sleep?
6. When do you clean your apartment?
7. Where did you take your grandchildren?
8. What did you make for dinner?
9. When does Carla read her e-mail?
10. When did you get up today?

Page 129 Exercise B

Listen and circle the word you hear.

1. My husband is thin.
2. She was very hungry.
3. They were tired today.
4. He was very energetic at school today.
5. My wife is at the clinic.
6. Their clothes were clean.
7. My children are very sick today.
8. My parents are home tonight.
9. He was very full this morning.
10. The Lopez family is on vacation.
11. Their neighbors are very noisy.
12. These clothes were dirty.

Page 131 Exercise E

Listen and circle the word you hear.

1. I wasn't busy yesterday.
2. We were at the movies last night.
3. They weren't home today.
4. Tom was on time for his plane.
5. It wasn't cold yesterday.
6. They weren't at the baseball game.
7. My friends were late for the party.
8. The doctor was in her office at noon.

Page 134 Exercise I

Listen and choose the correct response.

1. Where were you born?
2. Where did you grow up?
3. What was your favorite subject in school?
4. When did you move here?
5. What did you look like when you were young?
6. Did you have freckles?
7. What do you do in your spare time?
8. Did you have a favorite hero?

Page 137 Exercise F

Listen and circle the word you hear.

Ex. Is Jane rich or poor?

1. It was a nice day today.
2. My friends were thirsty at lunch.
3. Who is your favorite hero?
4. Were Mr. and Mrs. Parker at home last weekend?
5. My new couch is uncomfortable.
6. My cousins were late for their plane.
7. Before I met Howard, I was very sad.
8. Your children are very cute.

UNIT 1

WORKBOOK PAGE 2

A. What Are They Saying?
1. What's, name
2. address, My, is
3. your, phone number
4. your, name
5. What's, address
6. phone, My, number
7. Where are, I'm from

WORKBOOK PAGE 3

B. Name/Address/Phone Number
(Answers will vary.)

C. Listening
1.	5	6.	3
2.	7	7.	4
3.	2	8.	8
4.	6	9.	10
5.	1	10.	9

WORKBOOK PAGE 4

D. Numbers
4	2	six	eight
7	9	two	ten
1	6	seven	four
8	5	three	nine
10	3	one	five

E. Listening
1.	2	3.	6	5.	7, 3
2.	5	4.	10	6.	1, 4, 8

WORKBOOK PAGE 5

F. Listening
1.	R, E	4.	R, O
2.	H, S, N	5.	P, L
3.	G, A, D	6.	M, T, Z

G. What Are They Saying?
1. name
2. Hi
3. meet
4. Nice
5. you
6. My
7. is
8. Hello
9. I'm
10. to
11. you

UNIT 2

WORKBOOK PAGE 6

A. Puzzle

B. Listening
1. ✔ ___   2. ___ ✔   3. ✔ ___
4. ✔ ___   5. ___ ✔   6. ✔ ___

WORKBOOK PAGE 7

C. What Are They Saying?
1. Where, I'm, bedroom
2. are, They're, yard
3. are, We're, kitchen
4. Where, I'm, dining room
5. Where are, They're, basement
6. are, We're, attic
7. Where are, They're, living room
8. Where are, I'm, bathroom

WORKBOOK PAGE 8

D. What Are They Saying?
1. Where's, He's, garage
2. Where's, She's, living room
3. Where's, It's, classroom

E. Where Are They?
1.	They	4.	They	7.	He
2.	She	5.	We	8.	She
3.	He	6.	It	9.	It

F. Where Are They?
1.	He's	4.	I'm	7.	You're
2.	They're	5.	It's	8.	Where's
3.	We're	6.	She's		

WORKBOOK PAGE 9

G. The Baker Family
1.	in the living room	4.	in the kitchen
2.	in the bathroom	5.	in the bedroom
3.	in the yard	6.	in the garage

H. Where Are They?

1. She's in the living room.
2. He's in the bathroom.
3. They're in the yard.
4. He's in the kitchen.
5. She's in the bedroom.
6. It's in the garage.

WORKBOOK PAGE 10

I. What's the Sign?

1. PARK, in the park
2. POST OFFICE, in the post office
3. RESTAURANT, in the restaurant
4. SUPERMARKET, in the supermarket
5. MOVIE THEATER, in the movie theater
6. HOSPITAL, in the hospital
7. ZOO, in the zoo
8. LIBRARY, in the library

WORKBOOK PAGE 11

J. Listening

5	1	3
2	4	6

K. Listening

1. you
2. Ms.
3. We're
4. How
5. Where's
6. He's
7. on
8. It's

L. Matching

1. c
2. e
3. a
4. g
5. b
6. d
7. f

UNIT 3

WORKBOOK PAGE 13

A. What Are They Saying?

1. What, studying
2. doing, She's eating
3. What's, He's sleeping
4. What are, They're reading
5. What are, We're watching
6. What are, doing, I'm playing
7. What's, He's cooking

WORKBOOK PAGE 14

B. What Are They Doing?

1. eating
2. drinking
3. studying
4. reading
5. sleeping
6. teaching
7. listening
8. watching
9. cooking
10. singing
11. playing

WORKBOOK PAGE 15

C. Listening

1. ✔ __
2. __ ✔
3. __ ✔
4. __ ✔
5. __ ✔
6. ✔ __
7. ✔ __
8. ✔ __
9. __ ✔
10. __ ✔

WORKBOOK PAGE 17

E. What's the Question?

1. Where are you?
2. What's he doing?

3. Where are they?
4. What are you doing?
5. Where is he?
6. What's she doing?
7. Where is she?
8. Where are you?
9. What's he doing?
10. Where is it?
11. What are they doing?
12. Where are you?

WORKBOOK PAGE 20

CHECK-UP TEST: Units 1–3

A. (Answers will vary.)

B.
1. lunch
2. What's
3. singing
4. mathematics
5. meet
6. pencil

C.
1. in
2. reading
3. He's
4. watching
5. We're
6. Where's
7. doing
8. It's
9. What
10. and

D.
1. T
2. 8
3. 6
4. J
5. 7
6. 0

GAZETTE

WORKBOOK PAGES 20a–b

A. Fact File: Titles

1. Mr.
2. Mrs.
3. Ms.
4. Miss
5. Mr.

B. Fact File: What's the Nickname?

1. e
2. d
3. b
4. c
5. a
6. g
7. i
8. f
9. j
10. h

C. Build Your Vocabulary! Categories

Sports	Instruments	Games
basketball	clarinet	checkers
soccer	trumpet	chess
tennis	violin	tic tac toe

D. Build Your Vocabulary! Crossword

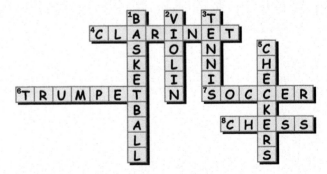

E. "Can-Do" Review

1. j
2. e
3. a
4. h
5. c
6. g
7. b
8. f
9. d
10. i

UNIT 4

WORKBOOK PAGE 21

A. What Are They Doing?
1. What's, cleaning his
2. doing, fixing her
3. What, my apartment
4. children, their homework
5. are, our sink

WORKBOOK PAGE 22

B. What's the Word?
1. my	4. her	6. your
2. our	5. its	7. his
3. their		

C. Listening
1. our	3. her	5. your
2. his	4. their	6. my

D. Puzzle

WORKBOOK PAGE 23

E. What Are They Saying?
1. Yes, he is.	5. Yes, he is.
2. Yes, we are.	6. Yes, she is.
3. Yes, she is.	7. Yes, I am.
4. Yes, they are.	8. Yes, you are.

WORKBOOK PAGE 24

G. Listening
1. he's	3. feeding	5. our
2. her	4. yard	6. washing

WORKBOOK PAGE 25

H. What Are They Doing?
1. washing	3. doing	5. painting
2. cleaning	4. reading	6. feeding

I. What's the Word?
1. They're, their	4. Where's	7. are
2. Where	5. our	8. its
3. He's, his	6. Is	

WORKBOOK PAGE 26

J. A Busy Day
1. restaurant	9. and	16. washing
2. eating	10. doing	17. his
3. in	11. playing	18. fixing
4. They're	12. laundromat	19. Where's
5. their	13. She's	20. library
6. park	14. her	21. What's
7. reading	15. are	22. He's
8. listening		

UNIT 5

WORKBOOK PAGE 27

A. Matching Opposites
1. d	4. c	7. e	10. i	13. k
2. a	5. f	8. n	11. j	14. m
3. g	6. b	9. l	12. h	

B. What Are They Saying?
1. tall	4. married	7. expensive
2. thin	5. small	8. ugly
3. young	6. noisy	

C. Listening
1. tall	3. easy	5. ugly
2. heavy	4. single	6. cheap

WORKBOOK PAGE 28

D. What's Wrong?
1. It isn't new. It's old.
2. They aren't quiet. They're noisy.
3. It isn't large. It's small.
4. He isn't single. He's married.
5. She isn't young. She's old.
6. They aren't short. They're tall.

E. Scrambled Questions
1. Are you busy?
2. Is your dog large?
4. Are they married?
4. Am I beautiful?
5. Is English difficult?
6. Is their car new?
7. Is she tall or short?/Is she short or tall?
8. Is he noisy or quiet?/Is he quiet or noisy?

WORKBOOK PAGE 30

G. Whose Things?
1. Albert's car	6. Mr. Price's house
2. Jenny's bicycle	7. Jane's piano
3. George's guitar	8. Mike's TV
4. Fred's dog	9. Mrs. Chang's book
5. Kate's computer	10. Alice's cat

WORKBOOK PAGE 31

H. What's the Word?
1. Her	4. Her	7. His
2. Their	5. Its	8. Their
3. His	6. Her	

I. Mr. and Mrs. Grant
1. Yes, he is.	8. No, it isn't.
2. No, he isn't.	9. Yes, it is.
3. No, he isn't.	10. Yes, it is.
4. Yes, he is.	11. No, it isn't.
5. Yes, she is.	12. No, they aren't.
6. No, she isn't.	13. Yes, they are.
7. Yes, she is.	14. No, it isn't.

J. How's the Weather?

1. It's warm.   5. It's cool.
2. It's sunny.   6. It's hot.
3. It's snowing.   7. It's cold.
4. It's raining.

K. Listening

1. cool   3. sunny   5. raining
2. snowing   4. hot   6. cloudy

L. What's the Number?

1. 24   3. 72   5. 97
2. 31   4. 46

M. What's the Word?

thirty-eight   ninety-nine   eighty-three
sixty-four   fifty-five

N. Number Puzzle

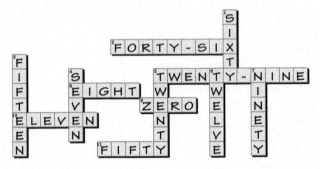

O. Listening

1. 86° / 30°   4. 72° / 22°   7. 66° / 19°
2. 32° / 0°   5. 93° / 34°   8. 34° / 1°
3. 81° / 27°   6. 56° / 13°

Q. Matching

1. e   4. a   7. f
2. h   5. i   8. b
3. d   6. c   9. g

UNIT 6

A. A Family

1. wife   11. grandfather
2. husband   12. grandmother
3. children   13. grandchildren
4. son   14. grandson
5. daughter   15. granddaughter
6. brother   16. uncle
7. sister   17. aunt
8. father   18. nephew
9. mother   19. niece
10. grandparents   20. cousin

B. Listening

1. ✓ ___   2. ___ ✓
3. ✓ ___   4. ___ ✓
5. ✓ ___   6. ✓ ___
7. ___ ✓   8. ✓ ___

C. The Wrong Word!

1. cheap (The others indicate size.)
2. park (The others are rooms of the house.)
3. baseball (The others are musical instruments.)
4. tall (The others describe people's appearance.)
5. dinner (The others describe the weather.)
6. rugs (The others are family members.)
7. bank (The others are classroom items.)
8. Mr. (The others are titles for women.)
9. poor (The others describe sound.)
10. sister (The others are male.)

D. GrammarSong

1. smiling   5. hanging   9. looking
2. living   6. dancing   10. hanging
3. living   7. having   11. smiling
4. looking   8. crying   12. Looking

E. An E-Mail from Los Angeles

1. It's in Los Angeles.
2. It's warm and sunny.
3. It's 78° Fahrenheit.
4. They're in the park.
5. She's reading a book.
6. He's listening to music.
7. She's Bob's sister.
8. She's riding her bicycle.
9. He's Bob's brother.
10. He's skateboarding.
11. No, they aren't.
12. They're at home.
13. She's baking.
14. He's planting flowers in the yard.
15. No, he isn't.
16. He's in New York.

CHECK-UP TEST: Units 4–6

A.

1. nephew   4. its   7. fixing
2. in   5. on   8. brushing
3. beach   6. reading

B.

1. Where   4. Who   6. their
2. grandmother   5. her   7. his
3. niece

C.

1. He's thin.   2. They're tall.   3. It's new.

D.

1. Are you married?   **3.** Is she young?
2. Are they quiet?

E.

1. b   **2.** a   **3.** b   **4.** b

GAZETTE

A. A Family Tree

1. d   **3.** c   **5.** b   **7.** a   **9.** b
2. b   **4.** a   **6.** c   **8.** c   **10.** d

B. Build Your Vocabulary! What's the Word?

1. opening   **4.** writing   **7.** raising
2. using   **5.** reading   **8.** opening
3. book   **6.** erasing

C. Build Your Vocabulary! True or False?

1. F   **3.** F   **5.** F   **7.** F
2. T   **4.** T   **6.** T   **8.** F

D. Fact File

1. father   **5.** brother-in-law
2. mother-in-law   **6.** son-in-law
3. husband   **7.** sister
4. daughter-in-law   **8.** wife

E. "Can-Do" Review

1. c   **3.** e   **5.** a   **7.** d   **9.** b
2. g   **4.** j   **6.** h   **8.** f   **10.** i

UNIT 7

A. Where Is It?

1. next to   **7.** across from
2. across from   **8.** around the
3. between   corner from
4. around the corner from   **9.** next to
5. next to   **10.** between
6. between   **11.** across from

B. What Are They Saying?

1. There's, next to
2. Is there, There's, around the corner from
3. there, There's, across from
4. Is there, There's, between
5. Is there, there, There's, Central, next to

C. Listening

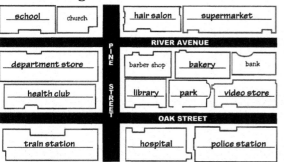

D. Yes or No?

1. No, there isn't.   **6.** No, there isn't.
2. Yes, there is.   **7.** No, there isn't.
3. No, there isn't.   **8.** Yes, there is.
4. Yes, there is.   **9.** No, there isn't.
5. Yes, there is.

F. What Are They Saying?

1. Is there   **6.** there isn't, there are
2. there is   **7.** Are there
3. are there   **8.** there aren't, there's
4. There's, there are   **9.** are there
5. Is there   **10.** There are, there's

G. Our Apartment Building

1. machines   **6.** satellite dish
2. broken   **7.** refrigerator
3. mice   **8.** closets
4. escape   **9.** cats, dogs
5. hole   **10.** stop, mailbox

H. Jane's Living Room

1. Yes, there is.   **8.** No, there isn't.
2. No, there isn't.   **9.** No, there aren't.
3. Yes, there are.   **10.** Yes, there is.
4. Yes, there is.   **11.** Yes, there is.
5. No, there aren't.   **12.** No, there isn't.
6. Yes, there are.   **13.** Yes, there are.
7. Yes, there are.   **14.** No, there isn't.

I. Looking For an Apartment

1. Chicago   **11.** New York
2. sunny   **12.** large
3. bedroom, bathroom   **13.** living room
4. fireplaces   **14.** air conditioners
5. children   **15.** school
6. Miami   **16.** Dallas
7. beautiful   **17.** quiet
8. bedrooms   **18.** dining room
9. two   **19.** building
10. elevator   **20.** near

UNIT 8

A. What's the Word?

1. tie   **10.** skirt   **19.** stocking
2. shirt   **11.** glasses   **20.** hat
3. jacket   **12.** suit   **21.** watch
4. pants   **13.** belt   **22.** glove
5. umbrella   **14.** sock   **23.** briefcase
6. earring   **15.** shoe   **24.** mitten
7. necklace   **16.** dress   **25.** sweater
8. blouse   **17.** coat   **26.** jeans
9. bracelet   **18.** purse   **27.** boot

B. *A or An?*

1. a	7. a	13. an	19. an
2. an	8. an	14. a	20. an
3. a	9. an	15. a	21. a
4. an	10. a	16. a	22. an
5. a	11. a	17. an	23. a
6. an	12. a	18. a	24. a

C. Singular/Plural

1. a hat	7. a glove	13. nieces
2. a basement	8. socks	14. women
3. dresses	9. drums	15. a child
4. bosses	10. a room	16. mice
5. exercises	11. earrings	17. a tooth
6. a watch	12. a purse	18. a person

D. Listening

1. umbrellas	9. necklaces
2. blouses	10. earring
3. coats	11. belt
4. computer	12. watches
5. shoes	13. nieces
6. exercises	14. nephew
7. dress	15. shirts
8. restaurants	16. tie

E. Listening

1. blue	3. gray	5. yellow
2. green	4. silver	6. orange

G. What Are They Looking For?

1. a pair of pants	6. a pair of boots
2. a pair of gloves	7. a pair of stockings
3. a pair of shoes	8. a pair of earrings
4. a pair of jeans	9. a pair of pajamas
5. a pair of mittens	

H. Listening

1. ___ ✔	2. ✔ ___
3. ___ ✔	4. ___ ✔
5. ✔ ___	6. ___ ✔
7. ✔ ___	8. ___ ✔

I. Listening

1. is	4. is	7. is
2. are	5. are	8. are
3. are	6. are	9. is

J. This/That/These/Those

1. This hat is orange.
2. That hat is yellow.
3. These boots are brown.
4. Those boots are black.
5. This computer is expensive.
6. That computer is cheap.

7. These gloves are small.
8. Those gloves are large.
9. This tie is pretty.
10. That tie is ugly.
11. These earrings are gold.
12. Those earrings are silver.

K. Singular → Plural

1. Those coats are blue.
2. These bracelets are new.
3. Those watches are beautiful.
4. These are Tom's jackets.
5. These aren't your shoes.
6. Are those your earrings?
7. Those aren't your notebooks.
8. These people aren't rich.

L. Plural → Singular

1. This sweater is pretty.
2. That purse is expensive.
3. Is this your neighbor?
4. Is that your dress?
5. That's Bill's shirt.
6. This woman is my friend.
7. This isn't my glove.
8. That's her cat

M. Scrambled Sentences

1. I think that's my jacket.
2. These are my new gloves.
3. Those aren't your black boots.
4. Blue suits are very popular this year.
5. Here's a nice pair of sunglasses.
6. That's my brother's old car.

P. This/That/These/Those

1. This, These, this	4. those, that
2. That, those	5. This, This, these
3. This, This, these	6. those, that

Q. GrammarSong

1. this	10. This	19. are
2. this	11. that	20. these
3. shirt	12. This	21. those
4. That's	13. that	22. This
5. skirt	14. these	23. that
6. this	15. Are	24. These
7. hat	16. boots	25. those
8. this	17. Those	26. that
9. that	18. suits	

CHECK-UP TEST: Units 7–8

A.

1. these	5. How
2. of	6. people
3. Is there	7. there
4. earring	8. No, there isn't.

B.

1. It's around the corner from the barber shop.
2. It's across from the library.
3. It's between the clinic and the drug store.

C.

1. their (The others are demonstratives.)
2. striped (The others are colors.)
3. closet (The others are places in the community.)
4. necklace (The others are worn on the feet.)

D.

1. These gloves are large.
2. That table is broken.
3. Those shoes are black.

E.

1. These rooms are small.
2. Those aren't my pencils.
3. Are these your boots?

F.

1. is   2. are   3. are   4. is

GAZETTE

WORKBOOK PAGES 61a–b

A. Clothing, Colors, and Cultures

1. c	3. a	5. c
2. d	4. b	6. d

B. Build Your Vocabulary! Crossword

C. Fact File: Urban, Suburban, and Rural Areas

1. a	3. a	5. c
2. c	4. b	6. b

E. "Can-Do" Review

1. f	3. a	5. c	7. d	9. g
2. j	4. h	6. i	8. b	10. e

UNIT 9

WORKBOOK PAGES 62–63

A. Interviews Around the World

1. What's	8. language	15. Our
2. name	9. speak	16. names
3. is	10. do	17. do
4. do	11. you	18. you
5. you	12. eat	19. We
6. live	13. watch	20. live
7. What	14. are	21. What

22. do	32. Their	41. do
23. you	33. names	42. they
24. speak	34. are	43. speak
25. do	35. Where	44. do
26. do	36. do	45. do
27. we	37. They	46. they
28. sing	38. live	47. eat
29. read	39. What	48. they
30. What	40. language	49. watch
31. are		

B. Listening

1. a	3. a	5. b
2. b	4. a	6. b

WORKBOOK PAGES 63–64

C. People Around the World

1. Her name is Jane.
2. She lives in Montreal.
3. She plays the piano, and she listens to Canadian music.
4. What's his name?
5. Where does he live?
6. He speaks Arabic.
7. does he do
   eats, he reads Egyptian newspapers
8. Her name is Sonia.
9. Where does
   She lives in Sao Paulo.
10. does she speak
    She speaks Portuguese.
11. does she do
    She does exercises, and she plays soccer.

WORKBOOK PAGE 66

F. Eduardo's Family

1. live	7. reads	12. shop
2. speak	8. works	13. plays
3. speaks	9. cook	14. play
4. speak	10. work	15. do
5. read	11. clean	16. do
6. live		

G. Listening

1. live	4. listen	7. sing
2. do	5. watches	8. eats
3. does	6. eat	9. reads

WORKBOOK PAGE 67

H. What's the Word?

1. does, lives   4. do, live
2. do, paint   5. do, cook
3. does, drives   6. does, do, sells

I. What's the Difference?

1. drives	3. plays	5. paints
2. work	4. sells	6. lives

WORKBOOK PAGE 68

K. Loud and Clear

1. Charlie, chair, kitchen, Chinese
2. Shirley, short, shoes

(continued)

3. Richard, cheap, French, watch
4. washing, shirt, washing machine
5. Chen, children, bench, church
6. Sharp, English, station

UNIT 10

WORKBOOK PAGE 69

A. What's the Day?

1.	Tuesday	3.	Wednesday	5.	Friday
2.	Saturday	4.	Sunday	6.	Monday

B. What Are They Saying?

1. Does, he does
2. Does, she does
3. Does, he doesn't
4. What kind of
5. Does, doesn't
6. Does, he does
7. Does, she doesn't
8. When

WORKBOOK PAGE 70

C. What Are They Saying?

1. Do, I do
2. Do, they don't
3. Do, we do
4. Do, we don't
5. Do, I don't
6. Do, they do

D. Listening

1.	b	4.	a	7.	b
2.	c	5.	c	8.	c
3.	b	6.	a	9.	a

WORKBOOK PAGE 71

E. Yes and No

1. doesn't cook
2. doesn't drive
3. don't play
4. don't work
5. doesn't live
6. don't exercise
7. goes
8. shop
9. wears
10. speaks
11. doesn't sing

F. What's the Word?

1.	do	6.	does	11.	does
2.	does	7.	Do	12.	does
3.	do	8.	Does	13.	do
4.	does	9.	do		
5.	do	10.	Do		

WORKBOOK PAGE 72

H. Yes or No?

1. Yes, she does.
2. No, they don't. They play volleyball.
3. Yes, we do.
4. No, he doesn't. He sings in the choir.
5. No, I don't. I see a play.
6. Yes, they do.
7. Yes, he does.
8. No, we don't. We do yoga.

I. Listening

1.	b	4.	a	7.	b
2.	a	5.	b	8.	a
3.	b	6.	b	9.	a

WORKBOOK PAGE 75

CHECK-UP TEST: Units 9–10

A.

1.	plays	3.	doesn't	5.	stay
2.	shop	4.	do	6.	does

B.

1.	Where	3.	Does	5.	When
2.	What	4.	Why	6.	What

C.

1.	lives	4.	plays	7.	goes
2.	does	5.	takes	8.	eats
3.	cleans	6.	rides		

D.

1.	c	3.	b	5.	c
2.	b	4.	a		

GAZETTE

WORKBOOK PAGES 75a–b

A. Language

1.	d	3.	a	5.	b	7.	d	9.	a
2.	c	4.	d	6.	b	8.	c	10.	b

B. Build Your Vocabulary!

1. hair
2. gets, gets
3. bath
4. brushes his teeth
5. takes
6. dressed
7. bed
8. work
9. gets up

C. Fact File

1.	d	3.	b	5.	a	7.	b
2.	c	4.	c	6.	d	8.	a

D. "Can-Do" Review

1.	j	3.	a	5.	b	7.	d	9.	c
2.	e	4.	g	6.	i	8.	f	10.	h

UNIT 11

WORKBOOK PAGE 76

A. What Are They Saying?

1.	you	4.	him	7.	us
2.	them	5.	them	8.	it
3.	her	6.	it	9.	me

WORKBOOK PAGE 77

B. What's the Word?

1.	it	3.	them	5.	it
2.	her	4.	him	6.	them

C. Listening

1. ___ ✔
2. ✔ ___
3. ___ ✔
4. ___ ✔
5. ✔ ___
6. ___ ✔

WORKBOOK PAGE 78

E. Write It and Say It

1. eats
2. barks
3. cleans
4. washes
5. jogs
6. reads
7. shops
8. watches
9. speaks
10. plays

F. Matching

1. c	3. a	5. b	7. d
2. e	4. g	6. f	8. h

G. Listening

1. b	3. b	5. b
2. a	4. a	6. a

J. What's the Word?

1. have	4. have	7. has
2. has	5. has	8. have
3. have	6. have	

K. What Are They Saying?

1. Does, have, doesn't have, has
2. don't have, have
3. have, have
4. do, have, have
5. Do, have, don't have, have
6. Does, have, doesn't have, has

L. What's the Word?

1. long	3. short	5. hair	7. suburbs
2. curly	4. single	6. brown	

M. Two Brothers

1. short	7. tall	13. plays
2. have	8. thin	14. play/have
3. has	9. he's	15. go
4. have	10. lives	16. go
5. short	11. has	17. watches
6. curly	12. in	18. reads

N. Listening

1. b	3. a	5. a	7. b
2. a	4. b	6. b	8. a

O. What's the Word?

1. in	4. in	7. in	10. of
2. on	5. about	8. to	11. to, on
3. on	6. for	9. at	12. to

UNIT 12

A. What's the Word?

1. sad	5. sick	9. nervous
2. tired	6. happy	10. scared
3. hot	7. hungry	11. thirsty
4. angry	8. cold	12. embarrassed

B. Tell Me Why

1. They're yawning because they're yawn when they're tired
2. She's crying because she's cries when she's sad
3. He's shivering because he's shivers when he's cold

4. I'm perspiring because I'm perspire when I'm hot
5. She's smiling because she's smiles when she's happy
6. They're eating because they're eat when they're hungry
7. We're shouting because we're shout when we're angry
8. He's covering his eyes because he's covers his eyes when he's scared

E. That's Strange!

1. cooks	6. dance
2. study	7. is sweeping
3. walks	8. are reading
4. brushes	9. I'm using
5. eats	10. are sleeping

F. What's the Question?

1. Why are you blushing?
2. Where do they play tennis?
3. When does she read her e-mail?
4. What kind of food do you like?
5. How many cats do you have?
6. What is/What's he using?
7. What kind of shows does he watch?
8. How often do you call your grandchildren?
9. What do they do every weekend?
10. Why are you smiling?
11. Where is she eating today?
12. How many sweaters are you wearing?

G. Which One Doesn't Belong?

1. we (The others are object pronouns.)
2. noisy (The others are adverbs of frequency.)
3. has (The others are forms of *do*.)
4. yoga (The others are emotions.)
5. Wednesday (The others are WH-question words.)
6. outgoing (The others are verbs.)
7. shy (The others are verbs.)
8. year (The others are times of the day.)

H. Listening

1. yes ☐	no ☑	7. yes ☑	no ☐
2. yes ☐	no ☑	8. yes ☐	no ☑
3. yes ☑	no ☐	9. yes ☐	no ☑
4. yes ☑	no ☐	10. yes ☐	no ☑
5. yes ☐	no ☑	11. yes ☑	no ☐
6. yes ☑	no ☐	12. yes ☐	no ☑

I. Loud and Clear

1. Sally, sorry, sister, sick, hospital
2. What's, scientist, speaking, experiments
3. cousin, Athens is always, busy
4. Sally's husband doesn't, clothes, closet

(continued)

5. Steven is sweeping, because it's
6. Mrs. Garcia reads, newspaper, Sunday
7. students, school sometimes, zoo, bus
8. son, plays soccer, friends, Tuesday

CHECK-UP TEST: Units 11–12

A.

1. him	3. her	5. us
2. them	4. me	

B.

1. feeding	3. baking	5. washes
2. goes	4. fixes	

C.

1. is	3. Does	5. Are
2. do	4. do	

D.
1. Where do they work every day?
2. When do you get together?
3. Why is he crying?
4. How many children does she have?
5. What are you drinking?

E.

1. b	3. b	5. b
2. a	4. a	

GAZETTE

A. Traffic: A Global Problem

1. c	3. a	5. a	7. d
2. b	4. d	6. b	8. c

B. Build Your Vocabulary!

1. walk	6. ride a motorcycle
2. bicycle	7. take a taxi
3. train	8. drive
4. ride a motor scooter	9. take the subway
5. bus	

C. Fact File

1. b	3. c	5. b	7. a
2. a	4. d	6. c	8. c

D. "Can-Do" Review

1. g	3. b	5. a	7. e	9. f
2. j	4. h	6. c	8. d	10. i

UNIT 13

A. Can or Can't?

1. can't ski, can skate
2. can sing, can't dance
3. can paint, can't paint
4. can't speak, can speak
5. can cook, can't cook
6. can't use, can use
7. can't play, can play
8. can drive, can't drive

C. What's the Question?

1. Can he cook?	4. Can you drive a bus?
2. Can she ski?	5. Can he skate?
3. Can they swim?	6. Can you play baseball?

D. Listening

1. can	5. can't	9. can't
2. can't	6. can	10. can
3. can	7. can't	11. can't
4. can	8. can	12. can

E. Puzzle

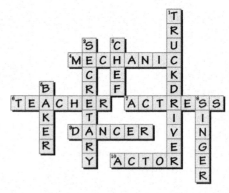

F. Can or Can't?

1. can	5. can	9. can't, can't
2. can't	6. can't	10. can, can, can
3. Can, can	7. Can, can	11. can't, can't
4. can't	8. can	

H. What Are They Saying?

1. have to
2. has to
3. has to
4. have to, have to
5. Does, have to, does, has to
6. Do, have to, don't
7. have to
8. have to

I. A Busy Family

1. He has to speak to the superintendent.
2. She has to meet with Danny's teacher.
3. They have to go to the doctor.
4. He has to fix the car.
5. She has to go to the dentist.
6. She has to baby-sit.
7. They have to clean the apartment.
8. They have to plant flowers in the yard.

K. Listening

1. have to	4. has to	7. can't
2. has to	5. can't	8. have to
3. can	6. have to	9. can

L. They're Busy

1. can't go swimming, have to go to the dentist
2. can't go bowling, has to baby-sit
3. can't go dancing, have to work

4. can't go to a soccer game, has to study
5. can't go to a movie, have to clean the house
6. can't have dinner, have to wash my clothes

M. Listening

1. a   **3.** b   **5.** b
2. b   **4.** a   **6.** a

UNIT 14

WORKBOOK PAGE 100

A. What Are They Going to Do?

1. He's going to cook.
2. She's going to read.
3. I'm going to study English.
4. They're going to wash their car.
5. We're going to play baseball.
6. He's going to watch TV.

B. What Are They Saying?

1. What are, going to do
    I'm going to
2. What's, going to do
    He's going to
3. What's, going to do
    She's going to
4. What are, going to do
    They're going to

WORKBOOK PAGE 101

C. What Are They Going to Do?

1. going to go
2. going
3. going to go
4. is going to
5. is going to go to
6. are going
7. are going to go to
8. going to, is going to go to

WORKBOOK PAGE 102

E. Which Word Doesn't Belong?

1. Monday (The others are months.)
2. September (The others are days of the week.)
3. at once (The others are seasons.)
4. Friday (The others are months.)
5. he (The others are object pronouns.)
6. next week (The others refer to right now.)

F. What's Next?

1. August   **3.** April   **5.** Sunday
2. Wednesday   **4.** winter   **6.** December

G. Match the Sentences

1. c   **3.** b   **5.** d
2. f   **4.** a   **6.** e

H. Listening

1. this   **5.** Tuesday   **9.** August
2. right away   **6.** December   **10.** wash
3. Monday   **7.** winter   **11.** next
4. cut   **8.** at once   **12.** plumber

WORKBOOK PAGE 103

I. What's the Question?

1. are you going to do right now?
2. is she going to baby-sit?
3. are you going next April?
4. are you going to clean it?
5. are they going to do today?
6. are you going to fix the doorbell?
7. is she going to plant flowers?
8. is he going to read his e-mail?
9. are you going to bed now?

J. Listening

Today's Weather Forecast

This afternoon: cool, cloudy
This evening: foggy, warm

This Weekend's Forecast

Tonight: clear, warm
Saturday: sunny, hot
Sunday: cool, rain

Monday's Weather Forecast

Monday morning: cool, nice
Monday afternoon: cold, snow
Tuesday morning: sunny, warm

WORKBOOK PAGE 104

K. What Does Everybody Want to Do Tomorrow?

1. want to   **4.** want to   **7.** want to
2. wants to   **5.** want to
3. wants to   **6.** want to

L. Bad Weather

1. He wants to go sailing.
    It's going to rain.
2. She wants to take her son to the zoo.
    It's going to be cold.
3. They want to go jogging.
    It's going to snow.
4. He wants to go skiing.
    It's going to be warm.

WORKBOOK PAGE 105

M. Yes and No

1. They don't want to buy
2. He doesn't want to go
3. I don't want to wash
4. They don't want to play
5. He doesn't want to cook
6. We don't want to study
7. She doesn't want to dance
8. I don't want to work

N. Yes and No

1. He isn't going to go
2. I'm not going to take
3. We aren't going to go
4. She isn't going to go
5. They aren't going to clean
6. It isn't going to be
7. He isn't going to listen to
8. You aren't going to buy

O. What Do They Want to Be?

1. What does, want to
   She wants to be
2. Where does, want to
   She wants to work
3. What does she want to
   She wants to bake
4. What does, want to
   He wants to be
5. Where does, want to
   He wants to work
6. What does he want to
   He wants to

R. What Time Is It?

S. Which Times Are Correct?

1. b	4. a	7. a
2. b	5. b	8. b
3. a	6. b	9. b

T. Listening

1. 7:45	5. 12:00	9. 1:45
2. 6:15	6. 5:00	10. 12:00
3. 4:30	7. 8:45	11. 11:30
4. 9:15	8. 8:15	12. 2:45

U. Alan Chang's Day

1. He gets up at 7:15.
2. He eats breakfast at 7:45.
3. He leaves the house at 8:30.
4. He begins work at 9:00.
5. He works at a computer company.
6. He eats lunch in the cafeteria.
7. He leaves work.
8. He eats dinner at 6:00.
9. He watches videos on his new DVD player.

X. GrammarSong

1. week	9. February	17. to
2. year	10. April	18. to wait
3. going to	11. July	19. day
4. In	12. September	20. month
5. summer	13. December	21. right
6. fall	14. It's	22. with
7. waiting	15. after	23. to be
8. I'm going	16. past	24. you

CHECK-UP TEST: Units 13–14

A.

1. want to watch TV
   we can't
   have to study
2. wants to play tennis
   she can't
   has to go to the dentist
3. want to go dancing
   I can't
   have to work

B.

1. are	3. are	5. does
2. Do	4. do	6. Is

C.

1. I don't want to teach
2. We aren't going to bed
3. She can't bake
4. He doesn't have to go to
5. They can't speak
6. We don't have to do

D.

1. going to eat
2. she's going to go
3. she's going to have
4. she's going to take the bus

E.

1. What's she going to do tomorrow?
2. Where is he going to play tennis?
3. When are you going to go to the zoo?
4. What are they going to study next year?

F.

G.

English __8:30__ Chinese __1:30__ lunch __12:15__
mathematics __11:00__ science __10:15__ music __12:45__

GAZETTE

A. Time Zones

1. c	3. d	5. a	7. b
2. b	4. c	6. c	8. d

B. Build Your Vocabulary!

1. c	3. g	5. h	7. f
2. e	4. b	6. d	8. a

C. Fact File

1. c		**3.** a		**5.** c		**7.** d	
2. d		**4.** b		**6.** b		**8.** c	

D. "Can-Do" Review

1. d	**3.** h	**5.** f	**7.** i	**9.** g
2. j	**4.** a	**6.** b	**8.** e	**10.** c

UNIT 15

WORKBOOK PAGE 114

A. What's the Matter?

1. has a cold
2. has a cough
3. have an earache
4. has a stomachache
5. have a sore throat
6. has a headache
7. has a backache
8. have a fever
9. has a toothache

B. Listening

5	1	8	3
4	7	2	6

WORKBOOK PAGE 116

D. What Did You Do Yesterday?

1. cooked
2. cleaned
3. painted
4. shaved
5. typed
6. rested
7. danced
8. shouted
9. studied
10. baked
11. smiled
12. cried

WORKBOOK PAGE 117

E. What's the Word?

1. work
2. played
3. brush
4. planted
5. cook
6. studied
7. painted
8. watch
9. waited

F. Listening

1. yesterday
2. every day
3. yesterday
4. yesterday
5. every day
6. yesterday
7. every day
8. yesterday
9. yesterday
10. every day
11. every day
12. yesterday

WORKBOOK PAGE 118

G. What Did Everybody Do?

1. He cleaned
2. She typed
3. They sang
4. We skated
5. She drank
6. He ate
7. They cried
8. They barked
9. He sat
10. She rode

WORKBOOK PAGE 119

H. Puzzle

I. Peter's Day at Home

1. He cooked dinner.
2. He baked a cake.
3. He washed the car.
4. He planted flowers.
5. He painted the kitchen.
6. He fixed the sink.
7. He rested.

WORKBOOK PAGE 121

K. My Grandfather's Birthday Party

1. listened
2. danced
3. sang
4. played
5. sat
6. looked
7. laughed
8. smiled
9. cried
10. talked
11. drank
12. ate

L. Matching

1. e	**3.** g	**5.** b			**7.** d
2. c	**4.** f	**6.** a			

UNIT 16

WORKBOOK PAGE 122

A. Correct the Sentence

1. She didn't brush her teeth.
   She brushed her hair.
2. He didn't play the violin.
   He played the piano.
3. They didn't listen to the news.
   They listened to music.
4. She didn't wait for the train.
   She waited for the bus.
5. He didn't fix his fence.
   He fixed his bicycle.
6. They didn't clean their attic.
   They cleaned their yard.
7. He didn't bake a pie.
   He baked a cake.
8. She didn't call her grandmother.
   She called her grandfather.

WORKBOOK PAGE 123

B. Alan and His Sister

1. rested
2. work
3. study
4. listened
5. watched
6. talked
7. played
8. listen
9. watch
10. play
11. studied
12. cleaned
13. cooked

C. Yes and No

1. Yes, he did.
2. No, she didn't.
3. Yes, she did.
4. No, he didn't.
5. Yes, he did.
6. Did Ellen clean
7. Did Alan talk
8. Did Alan cook
9. Did Ellen listen
10. Did Ellen watch
11. Did Alan study

WORKBOOK PAGE 124

D. What Did They Do?

1. bought
2. had
3. wrote
4. did
5. took
6. got
7. went
8. read
9. made

E. They Didn't Do What They Usually Do

1. didn't write, wrote
2. didn't have, had
3. didn't eat, ate
4. didn't get, got
5. didn't go, went
6. didn't drink, drank
7. didn't make, made
8. didn't take, took
9. didn't buy, bought
10. didn't sit, sat

G. What's the Answer?

1. he did
2. I didn't
3. she did
4. they didn't
5. we did
6. he didn't
7. you did
8. I didn't

H. What's the Question?

1. Did she buy
2. Did he have
3. Did you take
4. Did they go
5. Did you sit
6. Did I make

I. Listening

1. b	3. b	5. a	7. b	9. a
2. a	4. b	6. a	8. b	10. b

J. I'm Sorry I'm Late!

1. missed
2. had
3. forgot
4. met
5. got up
6. stole
7. had to
8. went

K. Matching

1. d	4. e	7. j	10. k
2. f	5. c	8. l	11. i
3. b	6. a	9. g	12. h

UNIT 17

A. A Terrible Day and a Wonderful Day!

1. were
2. were
3. was
4. was
5. were
6. was
7. was
8. were
9. was
10. were
11. was
12. were
13. were
14. was
15. were
16. was
17. was
18. were
19. were
20. was

B. Listening

1. is	4. was	7. are	10. is
2. was	5. is	8. are	11. are
3. were	6. were	9. was	12. were

C. Before and After

1. was, I'm healthy
2. was, he's happy
3. were, we're full
4. was, she's, comfortable
5. were, you're thin
6. was, it's shiny
7. were, they're clean
8. was, was, I'm tall
9. were, they're enormous

D. What's the Word?

1. Were, wasn't, was
2. Were, weren't, were
3. Was, wasn't, was
4. Were, weren't, were
5. Were, weren't, were
6. Was, wasn't, was

E. Listening

1. wasn't	3. weren't	5. wasn't	7. were
2. were	4. was	6. weren't	8. was

F. What's the Word?

1. did	10. was	18. Did	26. was
2. didn't	11. was	19. didn't	27. Did
3. was	12. Did	20. was	28. didn't
4. wasn't	13. didn't	21. wasn't	29. Were
5. weren't	14. didn't	22. didn't	30. didn't
6. were	15. was	23. were	31. was
7. weren't	16. was	24. Did	32. were
8. wasn't	17. was	25. didn't	33. didn't
9. Were			

H. What Are They Saying?

1. did	9. curly	16. basketball
2. were	10. Did	17. did
3. Were	11. didn't	18. were
4. wasn't	12. freckles	19. subjects
5. was	13. were	20. Did
6. short	14. did	21. hobby
7. did	15. sports	22. did
8. didn't		

I. Listening

1. b	3. a	5. a	7. a
2. b	4. b	6. b	8. b

CHECK-UP TEST: Units 15–17

A.

1. wasn't, was
2. were, was, wasn't
3. were, weren't, were

B.

1. was, I'm full
2. were, they're enormous
3. were, were, we're heavy
4. was, I'm tired

C.

1. didn't drive, drove
2. didn't arrive, arrived
3. didn't shave, shaved
4. didn't go, went
5. didn't read, read

D.

1. Did he meet
2. Did she ride
3. Did you have
4. Did they make
5. Did you see

E.

1. brushed
2. did
3. sat
4. ate
5. went
6. walked
7. bought
8. took
9. didn't take
10. didn't drive

F.

1. was	**4.** were	**7.** was
2. were	**5.** is	**8.** are
3. is	**6.** were	

GAZETTE

WORKBOOK PAGES 137a–b

A. Advertisements

1. c	**3.** c	**5.** b
2. b	**4.** d	**6.** b

B. Build Your Vocabulary! What's the Word?

1. messy	**4.** dark	**7.** fast
2. wet	**5.** light	**8.** high
3. closed	**6.** long	**9.** plain

C. BUILD YOUR VOCABULARY! Crossword

D. FACT FILE

Australia, Brazil, Canada, France, Germany, Italy, Japan, Korea, United Kingdom, United States

E. "Can-Do" Review

1. e	**3.** b	**5.** g	**7.** c	**9.** f
2. h	**4.** j	**6.** a	**8.** i	**10.** d

ACTIVITY WORKBOOK 1 ANSWER KEY: Pages 139–168

UNIT 1: Workbook Pages 139–140

B. Identification Cards

1. Gloria	**5.** Los Angeles
2. Gomez	**6.** California
3. M	**7.** 90013
4. Mexico	**8.** 2A

C. Address Abbreviations

1. Apartment	**5.** Avenue
2. North	**6.** South
3. East	**7.** Street
4. Boulevard	**8.** West

D. Writing Addresses

1. 31 S. Shore St.
2. 42 E. Central Ave.
3. 99 W. Lake Blvd.
4. 20 N. Main St., Apt. 8A
5. 128 S. Pond Ave., Apt. 2B

E. Numeracy: Numbers & Words

1. 26	**3.** 52	**5.** 61	**7.** 82
2. 70	**4.** 93	**6.** 36	**8.** 45

F. Numeracy: Numbers & Words

1. 418	**3.** 533	**5.** 442
2. 275	**4.** 612	**6.** 356

UNIT 2: Workbook Pages 141–142

A. Classroom Instructions

1. Take	**4.** Write	**7.** Raise
2. Put	**5.** Sit	**8.** Give
3. Go	**6.** Stand	

B. Classroom Instructions: Opposites

1. c	**2.** a	**3.** d	**4.** b

C. Numeracy: Adding Objects

1. seven	**3.** thirteen	**5.** fifty
2. eleven	**4.** twenty-three	

D. Numeracy: Word Problems with Addition

1. c	**2.** a	**3.** b	**4.** b

E. Continents and Countries

1. Europe	**5.** Africa
2. North America	**6.** Australia
3. Asia	**7.** Antarctica
4. South America	

F. Countries and Continents

Africa
Nigeria
Somalia
South Africa

Asia
China
India
Vietnam

Europe
France
Greece
Russia

North America
Canada
Mexico
United States

South America
Bolivia
Brazil
Colombia

UNIT 3: Workbook Page 143

A. Calling Directory Assistance

3	2
6	5
1	4
7	

B. Numeracy: Reading Telephone Numbers in a Directory

1. d	**3.** b	**5.** b	**7.** d
2. c	**4.** c	**6.** a	**8.** b

UNIT 4: Workbook Pages 144–145

A. Community Service Day

Circled words: cleaning, fixing, painting, planting, washing

1. washing	**3.** painting	**5.** planting
2. cleaning	**4.** fixing	

B. Numeracy: Word Problems with Addition

1. c	**3.** d	**5.** c
2. b	**4.** a	**6.** d

UNIT 5: Workbook Pages 146–147

A. Reading a Weather Map

1. foggy	**5.** 11	**9.** 80
2. 68	**6.** cloudy	**10.** partly cloudy
3. sunny	**7.** 55	**11.** raining
4. 12	**8.** snowing	**12.** foggy

B. Numeracy: Reading a Thermometer

1. 50° F	**3.** 95° F	**5.** 70° F
2. 10° C	**4.** 35° C	**6.** 21° C

C. Numeracy: Fahrenheit & Celsius Temperatures

1. c	**3.** b	**5.** f
2. a	**4.** e	**6.** d

D. Numeracy: Interpreting a Bar Graph

1. London	**3.** Hong Kong	**5.** Seoul
2. San Juan	**4.** Moscow	**6.** Rome

UNIT 6: Workbook Pages 148–149

A. A Family Tree

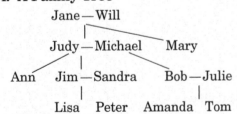

1. husband	**4.** aunt	**7.** grandparents
2. wife	**5.** brother	**8.** cousins
3. uncle	**6.** sister	

B. Numeracy: Adding Quantitites

1. two	**3.** three	**5.** twelve
2. four	**4.** five	

C. Numeracy: Word Problems with Addition

1. c	**3.** c	**5.** b
2. a	**4.** c	**6.** d

UNIT 7: Workbook Pages 150–151

A. Classified Ad Abbreviations

1. apartment	**6.** air conditioning
2. garage	**7.** living room
3. kitchen	**8.** near
4. bedroom	**9.** elevator
5. large	**10.** bathroom

B. Reading Classified Ads

1. three	**4.** is	**7.** $1300
2. is	**5.** stop	**8.** garage
3. isn't	**6.** supermarket	**9.** a stove

C. Numeracy: Word Problems with Addition

1. b	**3.** d	**5.** eight
2. c	**4.** a	**6.** eighteen

UNIT 8: Workbook Pages 152–153

A. Clothing Tags

1. Large	**3.** Blue	**5.** $12.00
2. $29.00	**4.** Small	**6.** Pink

B. A Clothing Store Ad

1. $65.00
2. $39.99
3. $19.95
4. $9.50
5. 6–10
6. $59.50
7. Small, Medium, Large, Extra-Large
8. $59.99

C. Store Receipts

1. $40.00	**4.** $135.45	**7.** $1.54
2. $89.00	**5.** $14.50	**8.** $40.04
3. $6.45	**6.** $24.00	

D. Numeracy: Word Problems with Subtraction

1. a	**2.** b	**3.** c	**4.** a

E. Numeracy: Store Receipt Calculations

1. 88.97	**3.** 6.59	**5.** 100.00
2. 93.41	**4.** 93.41	**6.** 6.59

UNIT 9: Workbook Page 154

A. Numeracy: Percentages and a Bar Graph

1. c	**2.** d	**3.** a	**4.** e	**5.** b

B. Numeracy: A Line Graph

1. 59	**3.** 76	**5.** 66
2. 35	**4.** 45	**6.** 85

UNIT 10: Workbook Page 155

A. Work Schedules

1. c	**2.** a	**3.** b

B. Numeracy: Word Problems with Multiplication

1. c	**3.** b	**5.** d	**7.** a
2. a	**4.** b	**6.** b	**8.** c

UNIT 11: Workbook Page 156

A. Describing People

1. tall and heavy; straight gray hair
2. short and thin; curly black hair

B. Numeracy: Word Problems with Mixed Operations

1. c	**3.** d	**5.** d	**7.** b
2. a	**4.** b	**6.** c	**8.** d

UNIT 12: Workbook Page 157

A. People and Places at School

1. d	**3.** f	**5.** b	**7.** c
2. a	**4.** e	**6.** g	

B. Numeracy: Percentages and a Pie Graph

1. T	**3.** T	**5.** T	**7.** F
2. F	**4.** F	**6.** T	**8.** T

UNIT 13: Workbook Pages 158–159

A. Job Interests and Work Skills

1. mechanic
2. salesperson
3. cashier
4. chef
5. building superintendent
6. security guard
7. waiter

B. Help Wanted Ad Abbreviations

1. part-time	**3.** evenings	**5.** required
2. full-time	**4.** experience	**6.** excellent

C. Reading Help Wanted Ads

1. c	**2.** b	**3.** d	**4.** c

E. Word Problems with Division

1. c	**3.** d	**5.** a	**7.** c
2. b	**4.** b	**6.** b	**8.** c

UNIT 14: Workbook Pages 160–161

A. Numeracy: Ordinal Numbers

1. 8th	**5.** 2nd	**9.** 13th
2. 15th	**6.** 60th	**10.** 31st
3. 1st	**7.** 10th	**11.** 24th
4. 90th	**8.** 3rd	**12.** 22nd

B. Months and Ordinal Numbers

1. sixth	6th
2. fourth	4th
3. seventh	7th
4. twelfth	12th
5. eleventh	11th
6. third	3rd

C. Numeracy: Writing Dates

1. July 5, 2018	7/5/18

2. April 19, 1976	4/19/76
3. March 22, 2015	3/22/15
4. January 31, 1994	1/31/94
5. August 20, 2020	8/20/20

6. Answers will vary.
7. Answers will vary.

D. An Employment Availability Schedule

1. T	**3.** F	**5.** F
2. F	**4.** T	**6.** T

E. A Bank Schedule

1. c	**2.** d	**3.** a	**4.** b

F. Numeracy: Elapsed Time

1. T	**4.** F	**7.** F
2. F	**5.** F	**8.** T
3. T	**6.** T	**9.** F

UNIT 15: Workbook Pages 162–163

A. A Medical Exam

1. Stand	**4.** Open	**7.** measure
2. Sit	**5.** Say	**8.** listen
3. Take	**6.** Get	**9.** check

B. Medical Appointment Cards

1. F	**4.** T	**7.** F	**10.** F
2. F	**5.** F	**8.** F	**11.** T
3. T	**6.** T	**9.** T	**12.** F

C. Numeracy: Math & Dosage Instructions on Medicine Labels

1. T	**4.** F	**7.** F	**10.** T
2. F	**5.** T	**8.** F	**11.** F
3. T	**6.** T	**9.** T	**12.** T

UNIT 16: Workbook Pages 164–166

A. Reading a Job Application Form

1. d	**3.** h	**5.** c	**7.** b
2. g	**4.** e	**6.** a	**8.** f

C. Numeracy: Elapsed Time & Amounts of Money

1. T	**4.** T	**7.** F	**10.** T
2. F	**5.** F	**8.** T	**11.** F
3. T	**6.** T	**9.** F	**12.** T

UNIT 17: Workbook Pages 167–168

A. A Supermarket Ad

1. T	**3.** T	**5.** F
2. F	**4.** F	**6.** T

B. Food Labels

1. tomatoes	**3.** Smart Shop
2. tomatoes, water, salt	**4.** Gino's

C. Numeracy: Supermarket Math

1. c	**3.** b	**5.** c	**7.** b	**9.** c
2. b	**4.** a	**6.** a	**8.** a	**10.** a

Correlation Key

Student Book Pages	Activity Workbook Pages	Student Book Pages	Activity Workbook Pages
Chapter 1		**Chapter 8**	
2	2–4 Exercises A–D	68–69	50–51
4–5	4–5 Exercises E–H	70	52
6a–b	139 Exercise A	71	53
6c–d	139–140 Exercises B–F	73	54–56
Chapter 2		74	57–59
8–9	6	76a–d	152–153
10–11	7	**Check–Up Test**	60–61
12	8–9	**Gazette**	61a–b
14	10–11	**Chapter 9**	
16	12	80	62–63 Exercises A, B
16a–b	141	81	63 Exercise C–66
16c	142	82	67–68
Chapter 3		86a–b	154
18–19	13	**Chapter 10**	
20–21	14–17	88	69
24	18–19	89	70–71
24a–b	143	90–91	72–73
Check–Up Test	20	95	74
Gazette	20a–b	96a–b	155
Chapter 4		**Check–Up Test**	75
28	21	**Gazette**	75a–b
29–30	22–25	**Chapter 11**	
31	26	100	76–77
34a–b	144–145	101	78–79
Chapter 5		102	80
36–37	27	103	81–82
38–39	28–31	106a–b	156
40	32–33	**Chapter 12**	
41	34	108–109	83–86
44a–b	146–147	110–111	87–90
Chapter 6		114a–b	157
46–48	35–39	**Check–Up Test**	91
52a–b	148–149	**Gazette**	91a–b
Check–Up Test	40	**Chapter 13**	
Gazette	40a–b	118	92–93 Exercise B
Chapter 7		119	93 Exercise C–95
56	41	122	96–97
57	42	123	98–99
58	43–44	126a	158 Exercise A
59–60	45	126b	158 Exercises B, C
61–62	46–49	126c–d	159
66c–d	150–151		

SIDE by SIDE Plus Activity Workbook Audio Program

The *Side by Side Plus* Activity Workbook Digital Audio CDs contain all listening activities and GrammarRaps and GrammarSongs for entertaining language practice through rhythm and music. Students can use the Audio Program to extend their language learning through self-study outside the classroom. The Digital Audio CDs also include MP3 files of the audio program for downloading to a computer or audio player.

Audio Program Contents